The "What Families
is designed to help you
tion, act with confidenc
sions when a loved one faces a health crisis. It is
based on the premise that the quality of life of the
patient and family always comes first.

Experts praise
STROKES:
WHAT FAMILIES SHOULD KNOW

Also by Elaine Fantle Shimberg:

RELIEF FROM IBS

STROKES:

What Families Should Know

Elaine Fantle Shimberg

BALLANTINE BOOKS • NEW YORK

Library of Congress Catalog Card Number: 90-91843

ISBN 0-345-36209-8

Manufactured in the United States of America

First Edition: November 1990

To my mother,
Alfreda Edelson Fantle
and
my sister,
Kay Fantle Arkin
and to my late beloved brother,
Charles Edelson Fantle,
known as ''Chuck,''
who taught me
patience and priorities

Table of Contents

sure? . . . When they're home, but not alone . . . Returning to the family . . . Expect some changes . . . It's not easy

has to offer . . . Developing an emergency corps . . .
Communicating with others . . . Helping yourself . . .
Accepting plateaus . . . Allowing yourself to be happy

Preface

Stroke! *Stedman's Medical Dictionary* defines it as "a blow; coup; hence, a sudden attack." And it is. Like an executioner's sword, a cerebrovascular accident, or CVA (stroke), can fell the sturdiest among us, swiftly altering the course and quality of life of its victim and creating rippling effects that engulf the entire family.

Although most families want to help their loved ones, they often don't totally understand the disorder or its ramifications, nor do they have any idea of how to behave toward the person who's been stricken and is acting so strangely. The medical terms are baffling, the shock of the abrupt onset of the illness numbing, and the stress resulting from a sudden shift of equilibrium envelops the family members like a choking smog.

I know. I experienced this firsthand. Summer of 1988, I kissed my active and alert eighty-year-old mother good-bye as I was about to leave for a two-week vacation. We talked about going car shopping for her upon my return.

"I think I want a bright red one this time," she said.

We laughed. I kissed her again. I felt strangely reluctant to leave.

Two days later, at one in the morning, I received a call from my brother. "It's Mother," he said. "She's had a stroke."

My family, like almost every other, has coped with many illnesses. We've overcome cancer, heart attacks, severe arthritis, numerous surgeries, and rheumatic fever. We're tough, my family. But I knew about strokes. I knew how they could bring you to your knees. Less than four years before, my father suffered a severe stroke. Now eighty-five, he resides in a nursing home, not recognizing us much of the time, not aware of the date or place, and requiring the constant care he receives from the dedicated Nursing Staff.

My heart sank. Was this to be my feisty mother's fate as well? Just at the time she was beginning to emerge with some acceptance of her new identity as neither wife nor widow, would she die? Would she remain alive, but not living? What quality of life would she have? Quickly we packed and made our way home, all my thoughts at the distant hospital.

As a professional medical writer, I have interviewed hundreds of patients and physicians. I have witnessed a child with cancer having a painful bone marrow extraction, watched women in childbirth, and observed complex surgery.

Yet despite all my background in the medical field and my extensive reading of medical journals and newsletters, I found myself at a loss when faced with my mother and her illness.

My first sight of her convinced me that she probably would not survive her stroke. She was barely conscious, was paralyzed on her right side, and was unable to speak. She had trouble swallowing and suffered from small seizures that caused facial tics. Looking down at her in the hospital bed, I saw the antithesis of the vibrant woman I had kissed good-bye just forty-eight hours before.

But the worst was still ahead. Ten days in the hospital were relatively easy for us, her family. We knew that there she was under the care of a proficient and professional medical staff. The stroke team—physician, nurses, and therapists—united to treat her medically, to teach her to swallow, hold a fork, walk, and try to speak.

My sister arrived from Iowa. We—my sister, my brother, his wife, my mother's sister, a niece, my husband, and I—alternated our visits. We came to the hospital, hugged and kissed her, noted who had sent flowers so we could write thank-you notes, quizzed the nurses about her progress, watched for any sign of improvement, and prayed. We lived in the today, not permitting worries of "What happens next?" to intrude into our thoughts.

The neurologist told us that we, her family, were an important part of the stroke team, but other than being told to encourage her, no one seemed to have time to tell us specifically what to do.

The day we learned we could take her home filled us, not with delight, but with fear. *We* were not skilled nurses, but then she didn't really require skilled nursing. She couldn't speak or write, but then we were her family. Shouldn't we *know* what she was trying to say? But we didn't.

We argued among ourselves as we devoured books about strokes—all of which told us in great detail what had occurred medically, but none of which gave us the kind of information we needed, such as how to communicate with her, how much to let her do herself before trying to help, whether or not to let friends visit, and what to let her eat. We felt as frustrated in our efforts to be of help as she did in trying to communicate with us.

For this reason, I decided to write *Strokes: What Families Should Know*. Although each stroke is unique, depending on what part of the brain has been damaged, the age and condition of the patient, and numerous other factors, some things remain constant. And while each family unit is different and pat solutions to all problems aren't possible, it does help to know that others have shared your experiences and to hear some of the solutions that helped others to care for their family members.

In preparation for writing *Strokes: What Families Should Know,* I have interviewed over one hundred stroke survivors and their families; physicians; speech, occupational, and physical therapists; nurses; and psychologists and members of the clergy. Their input has been invaluable and, I hope, will help to make this book a guide and comfort to the families of the over five hundred thousand new stroke patients each year.

Author's Note

The information contained in this book reflects the author's experience and research and is in no way intended to replace professional medical advice. Specific medical opinions can be given only by a qualified physician or therapist who knows the stroke patient, his particular medical history, and other relevant data. Always consult your doctor.

Acknowledgments

My special thanks to the many physicians and other medical professionals who shared their time and expertise with me. I am especially indebted to Peter Dunne, M.D., and Bruce B. Grynbaum, M.D. My thanks and appreciation also to my agent, Herb Katz; Anne V. Sasso, M.A., CCC-SP, Anita S. Halper, M.A., CCC-SP, Kate Brennan, RN, Santosh Lai, M.D., Robert J. Hartke, Ph.D., and Sandra M. Napolitan, ACSW, CSW, of the Rehabilitation Institute of Chicago; Sandy Samberg of the Howard A. Rusk Institute of Rehabilitation Medicine, NYU Medical Center; the Tampa Rehabilitation Center; Marion C. Kagel, M.A., CCC-SP/L, of the Crozer-Chester Medical Center; Leah A. Davidson, M.S., CCC; the Tampa Public Library; Dore Beach, Ed.D.; and Susan Folkman, Ph.D.

Special thanks also to my son, Scott Shimberg, for his expert help with the illustrations.

Many stroke survivors and their families were generous in sharing both their time and experiences. I have honored the requests of those who preferred to remain anonymous by referring to them only by age, geographic location, or career specialty.

The Holmes-Rahe Social Readjustment Rating Scale was reprinted with permission from the *Journal of Psychosomatic Research* II (1967): 213–218, Drs. Thomas H. Holmes and R. H. Rahe, Pergamon Journals, Ltd., and from Dr. Thomas H. Holmes.

1

In the Hospital

There is an old story about three blind men who were trying to describe an elephant. The first one touched the elephant's tail. "An elephant is long and thin," he said.

The second blind man patted the elephant's side. "No, you're wrong. An elephant is broad and hard."

The third blind man felt the elephant's trunk. "You're both wrong," he argued. "An elephant is thick and muscular."

Describing the effects of a stroke is much like that. Both of my parents have suffered strokes. Their stories are quite different. That's important to keep remembering. No two strokes are ever alike. You'll never know exactly what to expect. Even if you did, it wouldn't really matter.

When my father suffered his stroke, I was thirty miles away, attending, ironically, a seminar entitled "How to Stay Healthy," sponsored by the same hospital to which he would be admitted. Three and a half years later, when my mother suffered a stroke, I was also away, enjoying my second day of what would have been a two-week vacation in Maine.

There's never a "good time" for someone you love to be taken ill. No matter when the stroke occurs, you are bound to be caught off guard, either awakened from a dead sleep by a dreaded phone call or shocked by discovering the stroke victim yourself. Either way you're uprooted by the suddenness of the illness. Like the day John F. Kennedy was as-

1

sassinated, you'll always remember exactly what you were doing when the call came and how you were told. You'll replay it over and over again, as though by repetition you could change what happened. Dazed, you make hurried arrangements and head for what will be your main destination for days to come: the hospital.

For most of us, hospitals normally are confusing and intimidating places. When we're also under stress, even formerly familiar hospitals seem strange. Stretchers and wheelchairs speed by like cars on a busy expressway. We yearn to look yet avert our eyes, our childlike curiosity fighting our superstitious "There, but for the grace of God, go I."

Usually hospitals house miles of seemingly unmarked hallways filled with hordes of people—only some of whom are in white coats—running around and looking every bit as though they know where they're going. You feel as though you're the only one who's lost, as if it's the first day of high school all over again.

A few days later, however, it's amazing to realize how "at home" you feel in those same corridors, in the cafeteria, and within the structure of the entire hospital routine. You quickly learn the shortcuts through the maze of hallways, begin to call nurses and aides by name, and even recognize some of the codes constantly intoned over the hospital's loudspeaker system.

The Emergency Room

When you first arrive at the hospital, you'll probably spend some time in the emergency room, waiting until the doctors decide whether or not to admit the stroke victim. Often family members are kept in the dark, wandering aimlessly around the waiting room, wondering frantically if your relative is alive or dead, lying unconscious and alone in a forgotten room or being worked on, hooked up to science fiction–type machines. Your imagination runs away with you as you try to fill in what may be happening.

In some hospitals, however, family members are allowed to accompany the patient into the examining room, to calm him and help give the doctors and nurses important background information. For some people, this is hardly a plus: being there causes even more stress as they fight with their own anxieties concerning doctors, sickness, and even their relationship with the patient.

When my father suffered a stroke, I appreciated being able to be with him as he lay on a gurney in the emergency examining room. I stood by his side, holding his hand and chattering as though I could distract him from reality through constant conversation. It helped me to feel I was doing *something*, albeit not much.

However, I'll admit it also disturbed me when the doctors asked my father, "Do you know where you are?" I knew he was brought in by ambulance and wasn't wearing his glasses, so it was unlikely that he could possibly have seen anything in order to know where he was. I also knew that it was doubtful that he'd know the answer to some of the other questions they asked, such as, "What day of the week is it?" (I was so stressed that even *I* had to stop and think) and, "What's the vice-president's name?"

I didn't know how significant his answers were, but I knew the questions were being asked in order to determine how intact he was, how much damage had been done to his brain by the stroke. Like a nervous parent, I didn't want my father to "flunk" or appear stupid. I all but muttered the answers as I concentrated on them, wishing fervently that my father and I had better ESP between us.

I also found it difficult to stand by, patting my father's hand reassuringly, while a technician drew arterial blood to check the arterial gases. Because our arteries have thicker and tougher walls than our veins, I knew that it was a painful procedure. He moaned and begged me to make her stop. I wanted to slap her hand away, to yell at her to stop hurting him. I wished I could promise him that I'd protect him as he had me when I was little, that I wouldn't let him suffer any more pain or indignities. I felt both anger and helplessness, the first of many times I would feel that way, first with my father's stroke and then with my mother's.

If given the choice of waiting, uninformed and occasionally forgotten, in the waiting room of the hospital's emergency room or being in the examination room with the patient, I personally would choose the latter. It helps me (and, hopefully, calms the patient). I cope by understanding what's happening, even though emotionally it often hurts to know.

Sometimes, however, you do not have that choice. If your hospital's regulations require you to stay in the waiting room, you can still be assertive without being aggressive. (If you don't know the difference, check your library or bookstore for a good book on assertiveness and learn it.) Exercise your rights on behalf of the patient:

1. Ask for the charge nurse.
2. Introduce yourself.
3. Write his/her name down so you don't forget.
4. State the patient's name and how you are related.
5. Ask where the patient is, who is with him, and what is being done.
6. Ask if you can go in the examining room (sometimes rules can be—and are—broken).
7. If you have used a neurologist before and would like him/her on the case, tell the nurse.
8. If you leave the waiting room to go to the toilet or to get coffee, tell the nurse so the doctor can find you.
9. Remind the nurse that you need periodic updates on your family member's condition.
10. Contact the nurse for information if you don't hear anything in half an hour.

Always be pleasant. Be firm, if you need to, but a friendly tone usually gets you more response. Most nursing staffs are overworked and underpaid. They understand your stress and will make allowances, but try to work *with* them, not against.

If you are given the option of going into the examining room with your family member or remaining in the waiting room, take time to decide where you can be of most help to the patient. If you become hysterical or faint, you may frighten him more than alleviating his stress. Neither choice frees you from tension, of course. You're still in a state of shock, reacting to the situation rather than taking purposeful action.

Naturally you're worried, frightened, and fatigued and can't help wondering if there is something else you should be doing to help. But your exhausted mind refuses to focus. You rack your brain, trying to remember what it was you read about strokes—or was it something you saw in a television mini-series? Little, if anything, comes to mind, however. All you remember is meaningless bits of gossip about someone who had a stroke, and because it didn't apply to you, not then, you really didn't listen. Now you have all kinds of questions, urgent ones, fearful ones.

At the same time, however, everyone in the hospital seems to be busy doing his or her main job, which is to get the patient stabilized and to determine the extent of the stroke's damage. You may feel as though you're in the dark, that you're being ignored. "Nobody's telling me anything, and it's *my* loved one!" you scream in silence. On top of all the other emotions you're experiencing, you may also begin to feel anger and resentment at the treatment you're receiving. It's natural to feel that way.

As soon as possible, however, the doctor will come to tell you and the rest of the family what has happened and what the prognosis for recovery may be. Most physicians prefer to get the family together all at one time so they don't have to keep repeating the same information. Some doctors suggest placing a conference call to out-of-town family members at the same time. That way they, too, will hear the original medical report with the rest of the family and not feel so out of touch.

Why You Should Take Notes

It's unlikely that you or your other family members will understand everything you're being told at this first briefing. First of all, it's complicated information. Every stroke differs from another, depending on many factors—where the stroke occurred, what type of stroke it was, how much damage was done, the age and condition of the patient, and so on—so there is no simple way to describe what happened and what you might expect for recovery at this point.

Also, all of you are under a tremendous emotional strain. When you experience a shock such as this, the mind can't absorb a great deal of new information too effectively. It's as though everything has shut down, or at least gone into slow motion, to protect you.

Try to take notes, if possible, to help you recall later what the doctor actually said. If there are many family members gathered, don't be too surprised if each person gets a slightly different interpretation of the doctor's report.

What you think the doctor says (and doesn't say) is based on many factors other than just the actual words. Your previous experience in dealing with illness, your personal relationship with the sick person, your own health, the doctor's body language, and even how the physician talks to you can affect the way in which each family member interprets what is being said.

Also, because they are human, doctors differ in their ability to communicate complicated medical information to laypeople. Some physicians feel comfortable talking to the family and, although they may have little time between patients, can give the patient's family a sense of not being rushed. Others may seem abrupt and edge back to the door as they speak. Some may drone on in medical terminology, as though lecturing a class of second-year medical students rather than talking to a group of emotionally (and often physically) fatigued laypeople.

To be fair, it's also possible that the physician may have been up all night with other patients, may have just come

from performing lengthy and difficult surgery, or may have
an office full of other sick people waiting. Unfortunately it
also is true that many otherwise excellent physicians just
feel uncomfortable talking with the families of their patients, although they remain most capable in dealing with
the sick.

Nevertheless there are ways to be sure you are kept fully
informed about your family member's condition and that
you understand exactly what the doctor is saying. Chapter
12 describes in detail how to be sure you and the physician
communicate, rather than just talk *at* each other.

The Stroke Team and What They Do

The doctor probably will tell you that your family member is being cared for by a "stroke team." This is a spe-
cially trained group of professionals who care for stroke
survivors. The stroke team includes physicians, the nursing
staff, social workers, nutritionists, and therapists—physical,
occupational, and speech. Each of these therapists embraces
a different type of therapy, all of which are important to the
stroke survivor's rehabilitation. In later chapters you'll hear
more about these three therapy specializations and what they
do. You, the family, also are considered part of the stroke
team, as the patient's family plays a vital part in encouraging and supporting the patient on the long and often frustrating road to recovery.

When does rehabilitation begin? As soon as a stroke is
diagnosed and the physician feels that the patient is stable.
The therapists will work with the patient to learn his goals
and desires—which may range from wanting to return to
active employment to being able to return home to care for
a house and children or just becoming as independent as
possible, although in a wheelchair.

Goals are vital, as a patient needs strong motivation to
work through pain, frustration, and failures. Goals also must
be realistic enough to be reached. You too must be realistic
about what is possible for your relative. Often, because we

love them, we want them to be just as they were before the stroke. But you may have to lower your expectations. Improvement should begin after the initial trauma and swelling of the brain tissues goes down. Often a great deal of improvement is possible; sometimes, however, you may be disappointed.

The rehabilitation therapists shape their treatments to fit the patient's particular phase of recovery. Someone who is having difficulty in swallowing, for instance, may not feel too motivated to try to speak. All their energies are directed toward trying to keep from choking and drowning in their own saliva. The therapist works with that medical problem initially, easing into more speech work as the patient seems ready. Good therapy requires a great amount of respect, trust, and rapport between patient and therapist. The patient needs confidence in the therapist; the therapist needs to feel empathy yet remain in control. The therapist often acts as an interpreter for the family, explaining what is happening medically as well as therapeutically, offering suggestions and, often, just listening. No wonder stroke survivors and their families often feel quite attached to their therapists, especially their speech-language pathologist, and are reluctant to end their sessions.

What Kinds of Tests Are Run and Why?

Although doctors may differ on the types of tests they request for a stroke patient, most physicians make the diagnosis of stroke based on the patient's history and the findings on the actual physical examination.

If the patient is unable to speak, you may be required to answer questions such as "What medication does the patient take?" "Is there a family history of stroke?" "Did the patient smoke?" and "Has there been a personality change prior to the stroke?" Although it may be difficult to think clearly at this point, try to answer as best you can. Tell the truth. Don't keep secrets from the doctor. Physicians aren't judgmental. The doctor isn't trying to pry into your personal life but is asking these questions to gain important insight in order to make a proper diagnosis.

Blood Tests

As a person's blood can reveal many things, the doctor probably will order a complete blood work-up. The results will show, among other things, clotting time, the number of red and white blood cells, amounts of fat and cholesterol in the blood, and glucose level.

A CT or CAT Scan

Known technically as computed axial tomography, this scan of the head may also be requested by the physician. The CAT scan is a painless test something like an X-ray, which takes multiple pictures of the head that are then processed by a computer and show different levels of the brain, like slices. Tumors and hemorrhages show up as shadows on the film, revealing the size and location of the lesion. Sometimes the physician needs contrast studies, in which case a dye is injected into an arm vein and goes into the brain blood vessels.

EKG

An electrocardiogram (also known as an EKG) may be done to check the heart's function, as clots can be thrown off from the heart and enter the arteries of the brain. This procedure also is painless and noninvasive, which means it does not require penetration of the skin. A series of electrodes are stuck onto different parts of the patient's body—chest, leg, and so forth—and the machine prints out a graph showing the rate and strength of the heart beats.

Chest X-Rays

Most of us have had chest films taken many times. It usually is ordered for stroke patients to see if there is pneumonia or unexpected cancer or tumor.

Sonogram

This test checks the inside of the carotid arteries in the neck to see if they are blocked. It is a noninvasive procedure and carries no risk.

Arteriogram

Also known as a cerebral angiogram, this test is used to locate blocked or narrowed blood vessels in the brain. A catheter or tube is inserted into the femoral artery (located at the base of the groin) and worked up into the base of the neck, to the carotid artery. A special dye is injected into this tube, and X-rays are taken as the dye passes into the bloodstream and up into the blood vessels that nourish the brain. It outlines the veins and arteries, showing the areas of damage.

There is, however, an element of risk associated with this test, and there are many contraindications to its use, especially with those suffering from severe allergies, asthma or other breathing problems, cardiac problems, or extremely high blood pressure. The test itself can cause another stroke if the catheter carrying the dye knocks off a bit of hardened material called plaque from the arterial wall. Additionally, some patients are allergic to the dye that is used. Sometimes there is also bleeding from the wound caused by inserting the catheter. In some cases kidney problems may be created.

Why, then, with all the attendant risks, is this test used? Because it gives the physician important information on exactly where a blockage has taken place and how extensive the damage is.

If the doctor wants to order this test, he will discuss his reasons with you and the patient, if possible. You or the patient will have to give your consent, so ask the physician any questions you might have and express your concerns.

Additional tests may also be performed in order to determine what type of stroke your family member suffered and to assess the damage it caused.

What Treatment Will Be Carried Out and Why?

The first time you see the stroke patient in his hospital bed may be somewhat of a shock. Although he may be awake and able to communicate, chances are he'll be rather dazed and disoriented. His face may be slack on one side, he may be drooling a little, his eyes may not totally focus, and he may be unable to move one hand or leg or both. He may or may not be able to speak or even to understand what you are saying. The effects of a stroke vary widely, so it is impossible to prepare you exactly for what you might expect. With a slight stroke and little damage, you might see very little change; with a massive stroke and a great deal of brain damage, however, it would be a very different picture.

IV Line

There probably is an IV (intravenous) line leading from a bottle hanging overhead and down into the patient's hand or arm, where it is taped in place. This drip helps to maintain the fluid, nutritional, and electrolyte (chemical) balance until the patient is able to take fluids and foods by mouth. The line is also used to insert other medications into the patient without having to keep sticking him with a needle.

Catheter

The patient may also have a catheter, a tube passed through the urethra into the bladder to drain off urine. Men sometimes have an external catheter, which encloses the penis like a condom and catches the urine, which then drains into a bag. Most doctors avoid using internal catheters for too lengthy a period as they can create problems with infection.

As soon as the patient is stabilized, the doctor asks various types of therapists to visit and make their evaluations. Each discipline is different, yet all are vitally important in the rehabilitation process.

The Physical Therapist

The physical therapist determines the extent of dysfunction in arm or leg control and begins to work muscles—especially those in the arms and legs—so they don't stiffen. The goal is to maintain maximum mobility or movement. This is important since this skilled specialist works with the patient toward regaining or relearning many tasks most of us take for granted, such as standing, walking, moving from bed to chair, climbing stairs, and so on.

The Speech Therapist

The speech therapist, or speech-language pathologist, which is the actual title, also begins working with the patient as soon as possible so the stroke survivor can communicate in some manner and not feel so isolated. Many people suffer no loss of speech after a stroke, but for those who do, it is a frustrating world.

"I felt as though I suddenly woke up in Japan, without knowing a word of Japanese," said one stroke survivor. "Still worse, even the letters looked foreign to me. I couldn't read, speak, or understand what was being said to me. I've never felt so alone."

This communication problem is so immense and creates such frustration, tension, and sadness, both for the stroke survivor and for those who try to understand and make themselves understood, that all of chapter 8 is devoted to that subject.

The Occupational Therapist

Many people think the job of the occupational therapist is to teach someone to "weave baskets and make doilies." Actually it is far more complicated than that. These skilled people are creative thinkers as well, who try to help stroke survivors make adaptations so they can assume as much independence as possible. Occupational therapists teach stroke survivors to handle activities or daily living, known as ADL. This includes ways to feed and dress themselves using special button hookers, Velcro fasteners, swivel spoons, and other devices that will be discussed in chapter 9. They help the homemaker to relearn and adapt formerly simple tasks such as cooking and cleaning. The occupational therapist also assists those men and women who were in the work force to relearn or adapt skills so that, by working with a vocational therapist, they can return to work, either doing what they did before with some modifications or turning present skills and abilities into some other type of meaningful work.

How Can You Help?

As you stand or sit, holding your relative's hand, a thousand thoughts fly through your head. Will he/she live? Ever be the same? How will we manage? How will *I* manage? Why me?

Never feel guilty for whatever you're thinking. Strokes don't happen in a vacuum. They not only affect the person who suffers the stroke, but they also upset the balance of the entire family. *Your* life changed with the stroke too. There's no use pretending that things will be the same. They won't. They can't. You have a right to wonder how you'll be affected. All your so-called wild thoughts are normal ones under the circumstances. I've had them. Everyone who's loved a stroke survivor has too.

At this moment everything seems overwhelming. You may feel as though your reasonable, predictable world has gone out of orbit and is zigzagging on a crash course. Try not to panic. Take things in small pieces, day by day, and don't worry just now about major issues, such as how you will reorganize the house if your spouse can't walk, who will care for the children, and how you'll manage the finances. All those things must be addressed, of course, but not at this point.

Stay Calm

Although you may feel like wailing or screaming against the fates, try to keep from breaking down in front of the patient. You do need to express your feelings—sadness, frustration, anger, and the like—but wait until you've left the sickroom. Chapter 12 deals with the ways in which you can learn to deal with your feelings. You have to address them or they'll pop up in other physical or emotional ways. You can keep them buried only so long. Your loved one's stroke affects you, too, but you'll need a different type of "nursing" to cope with your specific problems. Just as the stroke team is designed to help the stroke survivor, there are professionals trained to help the family members as well.

Reassure and Reorient

Whether the stroke patient seems to be awake or not, explain that he has suffered a stroke and is in the hospital. If there is more than one hospital in your community, say which one and how he got there. ("You're at Doctor's Hospital. We brought you here in an ambulance.") Also mention the doctor's name, and if it is one unfamiliar to the patient, express your confidence in that particular physician. Identify yourself and any others in the room with you each time you enter, as visual disturbances are also common with stroke. Repeat this information often.

Inform

You can also tell the patient what's happened: "You can't move your left arm" or "I know you can't speak now." The person may not be able to understand you, but the sound of your voice should be soothing. It also helps to reaffirm the reality of the situation to you.

"I thought I was going crazy," one stroke survivor admitted. "They asked me questions, and I answered. Then they asked the same question again. Finally my daughter said, 'Daddy, I know *you* know what you're saying, but you're not making the right words. We can't understand you.' Thank God she told me. Just knowing made me feel a little better."

Touch

Don't be afraid to touch the stroke patient, to hold his hand or gently soothe his forehead or shoulder. The sense of touch is reassuring and may calm the patient, who probably is feeling very frightened at this point, especially if he or she cannot understand your words. Even someone who appears to be unconscious may be comforted by your touch.

Watch What You Say in Front of the Stroke Survivor

This is most important—so important that it will be repeated frequently throughout this book. Even a seemingly unconscious person can often understand *everything* that is being said. You may feel at this moment that "if she isn't going to be all right, she'd be better off dead," or "I never really liked Uncle Joe. It serves him right," but don't say so, not in front of the patient.

Don't Lie

Never promise the stroke survivor that he'll be "just as good as new" or that soon he'll be "running all over the place." He'll sense that isn't true and lose trust in whatever you say. He'll also resent your treating him like a child. On the other hand, don't express your worst fears. If the patient is able to ask questions, answer truthfully that "we just have to take things one day at a time. We all must learn to be patient."

Your body language is important, too, sometimes even more than what you say. Bobbi Baird, a professional singer, used her acting talents to express confidence to her husband that he would survive and make a reasonable recovery after a major and most devastating stroke.

"I lived in fear he might die," she said. "But I couldn't even admit to myself that I might lose him. I forced myself to be cheerful and perky, to touch him without breaking down."

Later, after his recovery, she asked him if he had ever thought he might die. "How could I have thought I would die?'' he told her in surprise. ''You were so perky! I knew you wouldn't be like that if you thought I was going to die, so I figured I wasn't in any danger.''

Encourage

What can you say? Encouraging words, such as ''We hope that, with therapy, you'll soon be able to tell us what you want. I know it's frustrating for you now.'' That gives hope while acknowledging the frustration you know the patient feels. You can also let him know that you feel frustrated as well because you aren't able to figure out what he wants. Trust your instinct. Be gentle, but keep talking. Often the sound of your voice is what's important, not what you actually say.

Speak in Short Sentences

Stroke patients are often very confused. Even those with no difficulty in comprehension may have difficulty following your conversation, especially if you speak in complex sentences the way most of us do normally. If there are others in the room with you and the patient, try to avoid crosstalking over the patient and getting so involved in your own conversation with the other visitors that you exclude the patient entirely. Save that for the coffee shop later.

Keep Your Visits Short

Strokes create a tremendous trauma, not only to the brain, but to the entire body. The patient needs rest in order to heal. If you've been in the room for fifteen to twenty minutes and others come to visit, say good-bye, gently soothe and kiss the patient, and say you're leaving now, but you'll be back. Then go. Urge others to make their visits brief as well.

Don't Talk Down

Remember that although the stroke survivor may be unable to talk, walk, or care for herself at present, she is not a child. She is an adult and should be spoken to as one adult to another. For some reason many of us tend to sound like our first-grade teachers when we talk with someone who has suffered a stroke. "Well, did we have a nice nap?" or "Don't we look pretty today!"

"I knew I had to get well," a stroke survivor told me. "I was going to murder all those people who talked to me like I was a baby when I was in the hospital."

Be Patient

You'll get sick of hearing this advice, but it's very true when you're dealing with a stroke. The brain has received an injury. It takes time for the swelling to recede, often as much as six months. New pathways may form to replace some of the injured, but this too takes time. You're not dealing with a computer that can be repaired simply by removing the back panel and adding a new circuit board. Progress for stroke survivors is often measured in baby steps, not in leaps and bounds.

Keep Informed

Ask for the charge nurse on the patient's floor and have him/her answer any questions you may have about the patient's condition, change of medication, or treatment procedures. Find out when the primary physician usually makes rounds and be there if you can. If you can't coordinate your schedules, leave a checklist of questions for the doctor to answer or a number where you can be reached. Most (but not all) physicians understand your concern and interest and will go out of their way to keep you informed.

Ask for Help

This is not the time to try to keep to your usual schedule. Leave Superman or Superwoman back in the phone booth and ask for help. Your friends probably have offered to do "something." Let them.

"Our daughter was three when my husband had his stroke," one woman recalled. "My mother came in from out of town to look after her, but it was a strain on me, having her there. We never had been close, and that lack of relationship plus the emotional tension I was under made those two months pure hell, for her as well as me, I'm sure. I wish my friends had thought to help with my child. I'm sorry I didn't feel I could ask them for that support.''

If you have young children, ask one friend to coordinate rides for school and activities so you can be relieved of that task. Your children, even little ones, will know that something is wrong, so teach them early that it's "okay" to ask for help when you need it. Allow friends to take over the "grind' work so you can spend what little free time you have enjoying the children.

Tell your employer that you may be late or miss extra days because your family member has suffered a stroke. Most people are very understanding and, if informed, can often help you reschedule your working hours around hospital visits.

Agree to have friends cook for you. If asked, request meal-type casseroles rather than cookies and cakes, which leave you "oversugared" and still hungry.

Don't Compare Notes

Remember that strokes affect people in many different ways depending on a number of factors, including what part of the brain was damaged and to what extent. If you compare notes with others whose family member also had a stroke, you may wonder why their patient is doing so well in speech therapy while yours can barely utter two words. You'll feel confused and understandably depressed.

Throughout this book, you'll read anecdotes about a stroke survivor and may think, "But this isn't like my wife,'' or, "Grandpa doesn't do this.'' That, again, is because every stroke is so different that it would be impossible to write one book describing every different combination of problems. By reading this book, you'll see some of the situations that you may be facing and will, I hope, pick out those points that apply to and can be of help to you, your family, and the individual who has suffered a stroke.

Note: Your final authority must always be those professionals who are part of your family member's stroke team, because they and only they can tell you exactly what is the specific problem and treatment for your particular case.

Keep a Sense of Humor

Laugh? Now? With my spouse or parent so sick?

Yes. Always and absolutely. Laughter reduces tension and makes you feel better. It heals the hurt, if you let it, by actually triggering the release into the bloodstream of chemicals in the brain called endorphins, creating a sense of relaxation and well-being. Hearty laughter, the kind we call "belly laughter," makes you breathe deeply, bringing more oxygen into your lungs. In his book *Anatomy of an Illness*, Norman Cousins describes how he feels that the power of laughter helped to cure him of a painful and crippling disease.

Although laughter can't alter the damage done by a stroke, it can help you cope with the days and months ahead. It can also reduce anxiety in the stroke survivor, who may feel that if you are able to joke and laugh, then perhaps things will work out all right after all.

Pace Yourself

" 'Patience! You all have a long road ahead.' That was probably some of the most important advice we received—and that we constantly forgot," said a middle-aged woman whose husband suffered a massive stroke that left him mute and paralyzed on his right side. "I wore myself out the two weeks he was in the hospital—running from work to the hospital, forgetting to eat, ignoring the kids, staying too keyed up to sleep. By the time we brought him home I was exhausted, angry at him for being sick, and angry at me for feeling that way. It made for lousy nursing!"

A neurologist who reviewed this manuscript said that "Have patience" was some of the most important advice he could give a family. "I had a patient who had suffered first a heart attack, then a stroke," he said. "I told the man's wife to pace herself. She was running around like a chicken with its head cut off, staying long hours at the hospital, then running home, then coming back again. She was trying to be all things to everyone. I pleaded with her to slow down. She didn't. Then she suffered a heart attack and died. The man, who had no one else to care for him, had to go to a nursing home. 'Pace yourself' is good advice. You're in for the long haul. It doesn't pay for you to get sick, too.''

It's almost impossible to understand in the beginning just what the doctors, nurses, and therapists mean when they tell you to ''pace yourself, to be patient.'' Most of us are used to illnesses where people get sick and require meals, bathing, and other tender loving care, but then recover and seem virtually as well as before. But with a stroke, everything seems to work in slow motion.

The brain has suffered damage in a stroke. Even in a minor stroke there is tissue swelling, just as with a twisted ankle or sprained wrist. Although medications are given to reduce the swelling, time is the great healer. Then new circuits must be formed, if possible, to take on the duties of the damaged areas. This also takes time.

Your relative will seem to make progress, then fall back. He or she may plateau and seem to be making no improvement at all. You all will feel discouraged. You'll feel as though life has become a roller coaster and you a reluctant rider. It helps to try to think of this plateau as merely a pause, some resting time. You'll find more in chapter 12 that deals with this frustrating aspect of recovery.

Take Time for You

It's hard not to feel as though you need to be at the hospital on as constant a basis as you possibly can, to show your love, concern, and support, to just be there. But the reality is that if you push yourself too hard, you'll burn out along the way. You've a long road ahead, and much of it feels like Heartbreak Hill in the Boston marathon. Not only does the stroke survivor need your support long term as well as in the immediate, but you also need to stay healthy for your own sake. You may feel as though your life is on hold, centered solely on the drama in the hospital, but the world is continuing to turn. You are part of that world, even though it doesn't seem much like it at this particular moment.

You may have other responsibilities—young children, aging parents, work, and so forth. You also have you. You have permission—not only from me, but more important, from numerous psychologists and physicians as well, to spend some time on yourself, to rejuvenate, to regroup. You'll be stronger mentally and physically and able to be of more support to your loved one if you take even an hour to go for a walk, see an exhibit in a museum, or just do whatever brings *you* comfort and peace.

One woman said she attended every one of her children's Little League games even though her father was in the hospital and only partially conscious. "I did it for me as much as the children," she said. "I always felt preoccupied when I was home with them, only half listening to what they had to say as I waited for the phone to ring from the hospital. When I was with Dad at the hospital, I made lists of what I needed to get for dinner, what the kids needed at the store, and what I *should* be doing.

"By taking time to watch my kids' baseball game, I was able to relax and unwind. It gave me something to talk with my children about rather than illness and my tensions and fears. It also made it easier to concentrate on Dad when I was at the hospital with him. A few hours 'off-duty' in the fresh air made me more focused."

Some people find it difficult to leave the stroke patient's bedside because they're afraid "something may happen." Of course, something also could happen even while they're on watch.

It's easy to let "patient watching" get out of hand. In some families it becomes almost a competition, with each relative trying to outstay the others in order to prove to the ailing family member that they're the most loving. Loyal mates exhaust themselves sitting for hours in the patient's hospital room or hanging over the bed, wanting to be there to reassure their spouse that they're there for them. But the watch takes its toll in fatigue, lowered immunity, and frustration. Nurses complain that sometimes it's difficult to care for the patient properly because they have to spend time shooing well-meaning relatives out of the room.

Be careful that you don't detract from the quality of doctor or nursing care. "I've spent twenty minutes in the patient's room, talking to the family, without even examining the patient," complained a number of physicians. "Doctors have limited time. They understand the family's guilt and anxiety, but they also need to spend time with the patient."

Try to limit your questions to the most pertinent ones while the doctor is making rounds. Either schedule an appointment or talk with the charge nurse if you need more time for explanations or have additional concerns.

Don't apologize for leaving your family member alone some of the time. He probably would thank you for it, if he could. Sick people need rest in order to make the best recovery. You need rest and some time off as well.

Get in the habit of making time for yourself while your loved one is still in the hospital and is being well cared for by the hospital staff. Believe me, it's much harder to take this "time out" once you bring the stroke survivor home, so develop the practice now. It will be even more important later. Chapters 11 and 12 both deal with ways in which to keep yourself strong and healthy while you help your family member back on that ever-winding road to recovery. Remember, be patient. Pace yourself.

=== 2 ===

What Is a Stroke?

Every stroke story, it seems, has its own unique beginning. According to *As I Am: An Autobiography*, actress Patricia Neal's first stroke began with a violent pain in her head as she was bathing her daughter. In her book, *Reprieve: A Memoir*, choreographer Agnes De Mille explained how she picked up a pen and noticed that she couldn't write. "My hand won't work!" she exclaimed. Physician Ilza Veith, author of *Can You Hear the Clapping of One Hand?* described how she woke up one morning to discover that her left side was paralyzed. In his book, *Episode*, Eric Hodgins reported feeling "under par" prior to his stroke. He was in the process of sending a telegram by phone when he suddenly discovered he couldn't speak. The telephone slipped from his hand and he fell to the floor. He did not, however, lose consciousness.

Although in retrospect it seems that my father must have suffered from a number of "little strokes" months before he had his most severe one—he had grown progressively confused and searched for words—his stroke revealed itself when he fell out of bed, probably trying to climb out to go to the bathroom.

My mother woke up as he called out and found him on the floor, unable to get up or to remember how he had gotten there. Although we assumed that he had had a stroke, neither my mother, brother, nor I had ever seen a stroke victim in real life. Our only knowledge came from what we had read in novels and seen on television or in the movies. His symptoms were far less dramatic, less specific. He could speak, although he was a bit confused. He was unable to stand or walk, although he could move his arms.

When my mother suffered a major stroke almost four years later, she was home alone, unable to speak or call for help. Yet she managed to walk into the elevator at her condominium, push the down button, and find the security guard, who called us.

Most adults have either known someone or have a distant memory of someone—often a grandparent or a great-grandparent—who suffered a stroke. For that reason almost everyone has a vague notion of what a stroke is and a stereotyped idea of what damage it can create. When asked, most people say, "It's a sudden paralysis," "It's when all of a sudden, you can't speak," "It's apoplexy, like when you've been struck down."

Although these answers may be true in some instances, they aren't always the case. Many people have strokes without suffering any paralysis at all. Others can speak, although they have difficulty reading or understanding what others are saying, or they may be unable to swallow, walk, or have use of one of their arms. Rather than defining a stroke by its symptoms, it helps to know what actually happens and why.

Most simply, a stroke is the result of a sudden blockage, caused by a clot, bleeding, or narrowing of an artery, that shuts off the blood supply to parts of the brain. As you may remember from high school biology, blood carries oxygen and nutrients to the brain, so when the brain is deprived of this vital blood supply even for as little as four minutes, brain cells begin to die.

Both times that I was faced with stroke and its effects on someone I loved, the neurologist patiently explained to me what a stroke was, what caused it, and what was happening inside my parent's head. A few hours later, however, I remembered nothing. It wasn't the doctor's fault—he explained things clearly and simply. It was just that I and the other members of my family were in a state of shock. We heard "stroke" and maybe a few other words, but because of the shock, nothing really registered. We weren't stupid; we were numb.

If you've had that experience, don't worry. It's perfectly normal. It's your body's way of protecting you.

What Is the Brain's Function?

Think of the brain as a giant control center, like the one you see on television during a space mission. The brain serves as a command post, issuing orders to the rest of the body.

When we want to pick up a glass, the brain tells the muscles to contract to move the hand and fingers. When we speak, the brain not only brings forth the words, like a computer calling up a word-processing program, but it also commands the throat, mouth, and tongue to move the proper muscles to form the words and directs the diaphragm to put the proper amount of air behind them so we can utter sound.

The brain stores information, sorts it out, and retrieves it as needed. It also controls our emotions along with our body and mind.

When everything works in sync, we tend to take our brain for granted. We may fuss a little when we forget a name, can't remember where we left the car keys, or have difficulty understanding the printed instructions that come with our kids' Christmas toys, but other than that we ignore our brain as we do our beating heart or filtering kidneys. It's just there, doing what it's supposed to.

But when a stroke occurs we suddenly realize how much a person's quality of life depends on the brain. Actions we always take for granted—swallowing, speaking, reading, walking, remembering—often become difficult, if not impossible. The brain is the person. Damage to the brain changes the person as we know them or destroys the person completely.

The carotid arteries supply the neck and head with oxygen and glucose-rich blood to fuel the workings of the brain. Illustration A gives you a view of the brain, with the blood vessels leading out into various parts of the brain like tributaries of some great river.

Illustration A

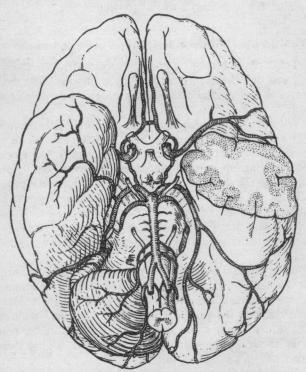

Permission granted by the Williams & Wilkins Co., Baltimore, Diane Abeloff, *Medical Art: Graphics for Use*, 1982.

You can see from Illustration A that the damming up of one of these vessels can starve the particular section of the brain it feeds, killing the cells there and thus damaging the work done by that specific area.

What Happens in a Stroke?

A stroke begins in a variety of ways. It usually isn't quite as dramatic as the movie version of someone gasping and clutching his heart or throat before collapsing.

The stroke victim may have complained earlier about being fatigued or just a vague "not feeling well." My mother had mentioned feeling terribly fatigued all May, June, and July before her stroke on July 11. We had assumed she was just reacting to the heat and humidity of Florida's summer and told her to stay inside in the air conditioning as much as possible.

Other stroke survivors recall periods of feeling dizzy, having a numbness in a hand or leg or on one side of their face, or having difficulty getting words out shortly before their stroke. You probably didn't think too much about it. You may have minimized the symptoms by saying, "You're just tired," or, "You really should slow down a little."

Don't feel guilty if you didn't recognize these signs of a stroke. It's hard enough for qualified physicians to be certain until they're done a complete examination and run numerous tests. You're not the first to be misled. It happens that way for many people.

"My husband called me on the phone," said a New York City woman whose husband suffered a major stroke. "His voice sounded slurred. I asked him if he'd been drinking, and he said no. He insisted on walking home, but when he came in he was weaving. He never lost consciousness, but I soon became frightened by his strange behavior. I called the rescue squad. *They* seemed to know it was a stroke right away. It made me feel so stupid for not thinking of it myself."

A man recalled his wife's stroke by saying, "She had complained of headaches before, so I didn't take this one too seriously, I guess. It wasn't until she dropped a plate and turned to me, unable to speak, that I realized something was terribly wrong. I couldn't believe she was having a stroke. She was only thirty-two."

Three Kinds of Strokes

Doctors divide strokes into three categories. Although the cause of each is different, all three types create damage in the brain. If you don't remember what type of stroke your family member suffered, ask the doctor or one of the nursing staff.

1. Thrombosis

If the doctor says this is the type of stroke your family member has suffered, it means that a blood vessel from the heart to the brain narrowed. This may be due to atherosclerosis—(also called hardening of the arteries) caused by high cholesterol and high blood pressure (also known as hypertension).

Calcium buildup and fatty deposits (known as plaque) on the inside walls of the artery to the brain caused by these conditions narrow the inside of the blood vessel until it actually becomes clogged, thereby preventing the flow of blood to the brain. It's somewhat like your plumbing pipes being clogged with a buildup of lime deposits or bits of hair or other matter so the water can't get through.

When the brain is deprived of its blood supply, cells die and the person loses specific functions performed by that area of the brain.

2. Embolus

This type of stroke results when a clot from the heart or fatty tissue from the wall of an artery breaks off and gets stuck in the smaller blood vessels that branch off from the major arteries as they lead into the brain. This clot blocks the flow of blood to the brain much like a pebble getting caught in a garden hose. The part of the brain served by the blocked area is damaged.

Note: Some physicians combine the two above types of strokes into one general category, calling it a cerebral infarction.

What cerebral infarction means is that a specific area

of the brain has been damaged because the blood vessels feeding that area have been blocked.

3. Hemorrhage

When this type of stroke occurs, it means that there was a weakness in one of the arteries leading into the brain. High blood pressure batters at the artery, finally weakening it until, at last, the artery bursts, like a balloon that has been overinflated. Known also as a brain bleed or a cerebral hemorrhage, this is the most dangerous type of stroke because it causes extensive damage as the blood leaks throughout the surrounding brain tissue. The blood also puts pressure on the brain, which can cause the stroke victim to suffer a tremendous headache.

According to Dr. Santosh Lal, attending physician and assistant professor at the Rehabilitation Center of Chicago, 18 percent of all strokes are hemorrhagic while 82 percent are nonhemorrhagic (92 percent thrombotic and 8 percent embolic). The nonhemorrhagic strokes offer a better prognosis, in that only 20 percent of those suffering that type of stroke die compared with 50–90 percent of those with hemorrhagic strokes.

How Is a Person Affected by a Stroke?

What actually happens to a person who has suffered a stroke depends on what area of the brain was affected by the clot or bleeding, the size of the lesion, and how much damage the brain sustained.

Each part of the brain handles a specific function—memory, creative thinking, speech, understanding speech and the written word, motor skills, and so on. When the brain cells in a particular area are damaged or destroyed, the specific function they controlled will be affected as well. Although other areas of the brain may pick up some of the functions, this can't be determined immediately, as doctors must wait until the brain's swelling goes down.

When the stroke causes damage to the right side of the brain, the left side of the body is affected, while injury to the left side of the brain causes paralysis and motor weakness on the right side of the body. There are also other problems, depending on which side of the brain was damaged.

When the right side of the brain is injured, the patient may have difficulties with spatial perception. He may suffer from memory deficits and show impulsive behavior. Often there is one-sided neglect, in which he doesn't realize the left side of him exists. He may catch his arm in the wheel of his wheelchair or wonder whose leg is beside him in bed.

The stroke survivor with a left-brain injury is more likely to suffer from paralysis or motor weakness on the right side, show cautious behavior, and have varying language deficits. The effects of stroke on people who are left-handed tend to vary somewhat and are often less predictable.

Illustration B shows at a glance the basic differences between left-sided and right-sided strokes. Remember, however, that each person's stroke affects them in different ways. No two strokes are exactly alike.

Illustration B (figure 1)

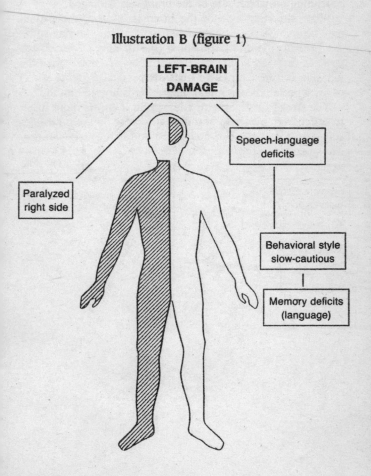

LEFT-BRAIN DAMAGE

Paralyzed right side

Speech-language deficits

Behavioral style slow-cautious

Memory deficits (language)

Adapted and reprinted by permission of the American Heart Association from *Stroke: Why Do They Behave That Way?* by Roy S. Fowler and W. E. Fordyce, 1974.

Illustration B (figure 2)

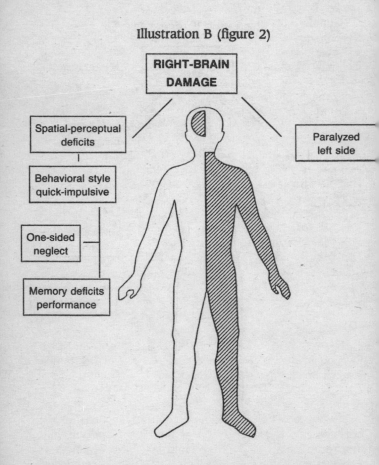

Adapted and reprinted by permission of the American Heart Association from *Stroke: Why Do They Behave That Way?* by Roy S. Fowler and W. E. Fordyce, 1974.

For more information on the differences between left-brain and right-brain strokes, contact your local chapter of the American Heart Association and ask for their booklet, *Stroke: Why Do They Behave That Way?*

Naturally, the first question you want answered after someone has a stroke is, "Will he live?" Once that seems probable, the next question is, "Will he be all right?" What you may mean is, "Will he be just like he was before the stroke?"

Although few people escape without some residual effects, doctors really cannot tell immediately how much damage was caused by an individual's stroke. They're not being evasive. It's just that until the swelling has gone down, it's difficult to evaluate the effects of the stroke.

In addition, other factors such as the patient's age, previous personal habits, nutrition, and general physical condition can influence the effects of a stroke.

That's why every stroke is different and why you can't compare what happened to your neighbor's mother with what is happening to yours.

Strokes do, however, have the potential of wreaking havoc on their victims. Maurice Levine, a Broadway musical conductor, producer, and writer, suffered a massive stroke in 1979. Now recovered, but requiring a cane to help him walk, he says of a stroke, "It's a little bit like a twister hitting a Quonset hut. The hut's never the same."

It's true. There are an astonishing (and confusing, to the layman) number of effects and combinations of effects that strokes can bestow upon its survivors.

Hemiplegia

Because one side of the brain controls functions on the opposite side (or hemisphere) of the body, a person with damage to the left side of the brain may have weakness or paralysis on the right side of their body, called hemiplegia.

Of course, there may be great variety in the type of affliction and in its eventual outcome or residual effect, once healing has taken place. It may range, for example, from the stroke survivor's suffering total paralysis of both his arm and leg on one side or just having a slight weakness in the arm.

Spasticity

Muscles in the stroke survivor's weakened arm also may become rigid (spasticity), causing the arm to curl up across the chest. Fingers may freeze in a fist position. Although physical therapists begin work immediately to prevent these problems from occurring, they sometimes happen anyway. Braces and splints may then be used to help support the limb.

Apraxia

Stroke patients with apraxia are unable to execute instructions. While they are physically able to touch their finger to their nose, for example, they are unable to do so when asked by the physician. A person with this problem is unable to carry out purposeful movement, but has no paralysis or sensory deficits. He understands the instructions, sends the message to the appropriate muscles, but they do not react. You may think he's just being stubborn, but he's not.

Ataxia

Ataxia is the inability to properly control coordinated movements. They can walk but find it difficult to begin walking when standing still first. The arms and legs seem to go off on their own, making the stroke survivor resemble a novice ice skater trying to maintain balance. These patients also tend to have difficulty making sounds and forming words normally. They may speak and sound as if they were intoxicated.

Aphasia

For most people, the left cerebral hemisphere handles speech. When a stroke affects that area, a variety of communication problems may occur. These difficulties may include an inability to understand what others are saying, an inability to use the right words, lack of reading and writing ability, and even the loss of former math skills.

Chapter 8 deals specifically with the loss of communication ability, as it affects not only the stroke survivor, but also his family.

Verbal Apraxia

Those who suffer from verbal apraxia have forgotten how to shape the mouth, lips, and tongue in order to say words. They know the words but are unable to get them out.

Dysarthria

Stroke survivors with dysarthria are unable to produce proper words or sounds because the part of the brain controlling the muscles that make voice and shapes it into speech have been damaged. These patients may also have difficulty with swallowing, as the same muscles control that act as well.

Visual Disturbances

About a fifth of those suffering a stroke will have some type of visual disturbance. The most common is hemianopsia, or the loss of vision on the paralyzed side. People suffering from hemianopsia may walk into a wall or chair because they don't see them on that side. Men may only shave one side of their face and women put lipstick only on the "good" side of their lips.

Double vision and rapid eye movements, called nystagmus, are two other possible visual problems that can result from a stroke.

Fortunately, no one suffers from every possible effect of a stroke. Those who do have difficulties may have them run the gamut from mild and hardly noticeable to severe and painful to observe. They all affect the stroke survivor's life to some degree as well as yours.

It's a strange new world you enter when someone in your family has had a stroke. The vocabulary is different and, in some cases, tongue-twisting. Doctors aren't always in agreement on the proper treatment. You often feel as though you don't understand enough even to know which problem to handle first. With all the illnesses in my immediate family, none has left me feeling more bewildered and insecure than stroke.

How Common Is a Stroke?

It is estimated that over five hundred thousand Americans suffer a stroke each year. That's approximately as many people as the population of Columbus, Denver, or Boston. Of this number, statistically a third will die within the first month, making stroke the third leading cause of death in the United States today (after heart disease and cancer). Over half of those suffering a stroke survive the first year, although about 90 percent will experience some lingering effects, ranging from as minor as a slight limp or weakness to total incapacitation and dependency. Stroke is the number-one cause of adult disability in America today.

But the disability isn't felt only by the stroke survivor. Almost all of those suffering from a stroke have families whose lives are also affected. Most of us handle things as best we can, but we often feel that we're whistling in the dark. As an artist and adult son of a stroke survivor said, "I'm hanging on by my fingertips. Everyone thinks *I* know what to do, but I don't. If I fall, my mother tumbles down with me. I'd like to let go of all the responsibilities and decisions. I daydream about how free my life was before my mother's stroke. Now everything has to be preplanned, arrangements have to be made for things we both used to take for granted, like grocery shopping, her weekly visit to the beauty shop, and doctors' appointments. I feel as though it were my stroke as well as hers. We're both victims!"

Who Is "Stroke Prone"?

Although stroke can happen at any age—and has been known to occur in children and infants—the incidence does tend to increase dramatically as we get older (over sixty-five years of age). Various risk factors have been identified and are important to know, even now, despite the fact that a family member already has suffered a stroke. There are two reasons for this:

1. You and other family members are at a higher risk for stroke because there has been an incidence of stroke in the family.
2. Approximately 10 percent of those suffering a stroke will have a second stroke within the same year.

By learning the risk factors that may trigger a stroke, you can change those things that can be altered.

Heredity

You can't do anything about your heredity, but you can take extra precautions against other factors that can be changed.

Age

Although strokes have been known to hit children and even infants, we all become more susceptible to strokes as we age, probably because of the accumulation of plaque buildup in the blood vessels. By eighty years of age, one in three people will have suffered some type of stroke incident. Although you can't keep from aging, you can become aware of those factors that can be changed and control those to help reduce your chances of suffering a stroke.

Sex

Men are two to one more likely to suffer a stroke than women. Although men are more prone to stroke at younger ages, women tend to catch up after menopause. Studies suggest that hormones may play a part in this, protecting a woman only until she passes beyond her childbearing years.

Race

Black males tend to have more strokes than their white counterparts. This makes it vital for black men and their families to become aware of those risk factors that can be changed and to begin immediately to put those changes into effect.

Diabetes

Men and women who suffer from diabetes tend to be at higher risk for strokes than those not suffering from diabetes, even if their disease is kept under control.

There's nothing you can change about any of the above risk factors. But these that follow can be controlled to varying degrees.

Smoking

More than one doctor has pointed to cigarettes as a leading cause of stroke. Certainly you should do all you can to support any family members—especially the one who has survived a stroke—in trying to give up this deadly addiction. But, at the same time, you should remember that smoking is just that—an addiction to the drug nicotine. It may be an exhausting battle to kick the cigarette habit.

Smoking probably is no issue while the stroke survivor is in the hospital, as most hospitals today forbid smoking in patients' rooms. The real fight, however, may begin when you get the patient home. He may think, "I'm going to die anyway, so what difference does it make?" or, "I can't work or even walk anymore. At least I can smoke."

Rather than creating tension between yourself and the stroke survivor by hiding cigarettes or refusing to buy any, seek professional help at the Stop Smoking Clinics sponsored by the American Cancer Society, the American Heart Association, or your local hospital.

Discuss the problem with the patient's physician and ask for additional suggestions. Don't be surprised if it's news to the doctor because patients often will say they have stopped smoking to "fool" their doctor. Sadly, they may be out-smarting themselves and end up suffering another stroke or even dying.

High Cholesterol

This is another culprit in stroke risk. High cholesterol means too much fat in your blood. This causes a plaque buildup, which coats the walls of your arteries, narrowing them and becoming potential missiles if they break off and head toward your brain.

Chances are, when your family member is released from the hospital, the doctor will give you (or whoever is cooking) a low-cholesterol diet to follow in preparing foods for the stroke survivor. Although this doesn't mean that the patient can never again eat an egg or a hamburger patty, it does mean that permanent dietary changes must be made in order to lower the cholesterol rate. Happily most people on low-cholesterol diets soon find that they enjoy the lightness of chicken and fish and complain of an uncomfortable fullness when they do eat a fatty steak or cheeseburger.

If the stroke survivor is an older parent who lives alone, you may have to bring food over or make other cooking arrangements until he or she becomes used to the new way of eating. Hopefully you are now cooking and eating with low cholesterol in mind for yourself and your family as well.

If the stroke survivor is able to go out and be with friends, discuss the diet restrictions with the friends in private before the luncheon or dinner date. Chances are they may be on the same type of diet themselves.

Don't be surprised, however, if an older person tends to fall back to previous eating habits. "I went grocery shopping with my eighty-five-year-old mother," a fifty-year-old woman reported. "She was good about buying chicken breasts instead of pork chops, and sherbet rather than ice cream. But she stopped in front of the cookie section and gazed at her favorites: chocolate sandwich cookies. I reminded her that they weren't on her diet. She looked so sad and mournful that I said, 'What the heck? At her age, she should be able to enjoy a few things even if they are bad for her.' I decided that if she was willing to take the risk, so was I.''

Lack of Exercise

Recent studies at Tufts University have found that proper diet and exercise can slow down many of the biological effects of aging. Much of the data shows that adequate exercise and low-fat diets can help to prevent heart attacks and stroke.

If you haven't exercised much before, now's the time to get a medical check-up and, if approved by your physician, begin. It will be good for you both physically and emotionally. Your family member's recovery from stroke is going to be a long process, with much stress and frustration along the way for the entire family. Throughout my interviews for this book, I heard time and time again that it was exercise that kept the caregiver going, both mentally and physically.

A twenty-six-year-old man, whose wife suffered a massive stroke just a few months after they were married, said, ''I run and play racquetball. I guess I take my frustrations and anger out on the ball. It relieves my stress. There's no use trying to drink your troubles away. They'll be there tomorrow.''

Stroke survivors need to exercise as well. This may seem strange to you right now, especially if your loved one is still in the hospital, with IV lines attached and yet unable to stand, let alone walk. But exercise and movement are important, even for a paralyzed person, who needs to be turned to prevent bedsores and repositioned to keep the limbs from stiffening. Those who must be in a wheelchair can also do special exercises. You'll read more about the importance of exercise—for yourself and the stroke survivor—in chapter 11.

Hypertension

Hypertension is another word for high blood pressure. It is a major risk factor in having a stroke because it forces the blood against the walls of the blood vessels like a hurricane-force wind battering against a sea wall. High blood pressure not only weakens the blood vessels themselves, but can also force loose bits of plaque from the vessel walls, hurling them free to do their damage.

Obesity

Excess weight creeps up on you before you know it. Too much additional weight places an extra burden on your heart and blood vessels. It also makes you more susceptible to diabetes and heart disease, both of which increase chances for a stroke. If you think that twenty extra pounds can't matter all that much, buy 2 ten-pound bags of cat litter and carry them all the way across the grocery store parking lot, searching for where you put your car, as I did. It's staggering—both figuratively and literally.

Poor Handling of Stress

It's impossible to avoid stress altogether. "Life without stress is death," wrote the late Dr. Hans Selye, author of the definitive book on stress, *The Stress of Life*. But poor stress management techniques can lead to increased high blood pressure, which can trigger a stroke.

Because the effects of stroke create more stress on the entire family system, it is vital for all members of the family—the stroke survivor included—to begin practicing various techniques to lower stress levels. These techniques will be discussed in detail throughout the remainder of the book.

Transient Ischemic Attacks

These may also be known as little strokes or TIAs. They may have similar symptoms to a full-blown stroke:

- weakness or numbness of the face
- weakness or numbness in one or both limbs on one side
- difficulty in speaking, understanding speech, or reading
- vision disturbances

The primary difference, however, between a TIA and a stroke is that the symptoms last less than twenty-four hours. Although many patients report that their symptoms lasted "only minutes," it is more probable that they lasted an hour or so, but were noticed for only a short time.

Because the symptoms of TIAs last only a brief time, people tend to forget about them. You shouldn't. *A transient ischemic attack is a temporary interruption of the blood supply to the brain and, as such, is often the precursor to a major stroke*. In fact, about half of those surviving a stroke remember having ministrokes or TIAs earlier.

Heart Disease

People suffering from heart disease are two to three times more likely to suffer from a stroke. That's why it is so important to follow your doctor's instructions in regard to diet, exercise, and not smoking. It can help prevent another stroke in the stroke survivor and can lower the risk in the other family members.

Using Oral Contraceptives

Women who use birth control pills are at a higher risk for having strokes, especially once they are thirty or older. Those who smoke as well further increase the risk of suffering a stroke.

Add up your stroke risk points from the Stroke Assessment Chart (Illustration C) and share that information with your physician if you are presently using oral contraceptives or are thinking about it.

Illustration C

Stroke Risk Assessment Chart*
(those listed in **bold type** are major risks)

FIXED RISK FACTORS

- **TIAs**
  (35-60% have stroke within 5 years)

- Atherosclerosis
  (hardening of the arteries)

- **Existing heart disease**
  (increases risk 2X)

- **Previous stroke**
  (increases risk 10-20X)

- **Diabetes mellitus**
  (increases risk 2X)

- **Age**
  (% of stroke risk more than doubles for each decade after age 55)

- Family history of strokes

- Race
  (blacks tend to have higher incidence, probably due to hypertension)

- Male sex
  (women "catch up" after menopause)

- Sickle cell anemia and other blood diseases

TREATABLE RISK FACTORS

- **Hypertension**
  (high blood pressure increases risk 6X)

- **High cholesterol**
  (contributes to atherosclerosis and heart disease)

- **Cigarette smoking**
  (increases risk 2X)

- Excessive alcohol consumption
  (increases risk 2-3X)

- Use of oral contraception
  (birth control pill) stroke risk increased 4-13X when used in association with hypertension, history of migraine, over 35 years of age, diabetes, or smoking)

- Obesity
  (which the American Heart Association defines as 30% or more over ideal body weight)

- Lack of exercise

- Geographical location
  (stroke risk higher in the southeastern part of U.S.)

- Poor stress handling techniques

Multiple risk factors increasingly pyramid the risk of stroke. For example, diabetes plus hypertension is more than twice the risk. Similarly, according to the surgeon general, a smoker who is taking oral contraceptives is 200 times as vulnerable to stroke than a nonsmoker. If you have any of the above stroke risk factors, see your doctor. Many strokes *can* be prevented.
*Information compiled from reports of the American Heart Association, National Institute of Neurological and Communicative Disorders and Stroke, and the National Stroke Association.

It's obvious from the list above that there are many risk factors associated with stroke. Some—like race, heredity, and sex—cannot be changed. But by being aware of all the risk factors, you can begin to alter those that are within your control. Remember that once a family member has suffered a stroke, all the family is at greater risk. Share your stroke assessment scores with your physician and follow your doctor's advice.

Once Someone's Had a Stroke, Can It Happen Again?

Unfortunately, the greatest risk factor in having a stroke is having suffered a previous one. Approximately, 10 percent of those who have survived a stroke have a second stroke within the year.

Can a Person Who's Had a Stroke Recover?

Most stroke survivors have some residual effects from their CVAs. But this doesn't mean that every stroke patient spends the rest of his life in bed as an invalid or dozing in a wheelchair or propped in front of the television set.

Rehabilitation can and has helped many stroke victims to participate in and enjoy life. Many, such as actress Patricia Neal, poet Walt Whitman, scientist Louis Pasteur, and composer George Frideric Handel, did some of their best work after their stroke.

After the Hospital

Although the actual length of hospitalization differs greatly depending on the individual and the effects of the stroke, most doctors try to release their stroke patients as quickly as possible, believing that the best rehabilitation can be made outside a hospital acute care setting.

Unfortunately few stroke survivors go home exactly as they were before the stroke. Most suffer from some degree of weakness, either a physical disability or some problem with speech, writing, thinking, or other mental processes.

For some, "going home" is delayed by a stay in a stroke rehabilitation center. For others, "home" will no longer mean one's own home, but, rather, a nursing home, where constant skilled professional care is available. Some stroke survivors move in with their adult children or other family members, while still others are fortunate to be able to return to their own home immediately and, with some accommodations, continue life largely as it was before the stroke.

There are, of course, a variety of other options available to the stroke patient and the family. The patient's condition, personality, availability of care, finances, home environments, and myriad other factors must be considered. There is no one "right" answer to the question "Where should the stroke survivor go?" and the decision that is made doesn't have to be permanent.

Before making any decision, the family should discuss all

the possible solutions with the physician, the social worker, therapists, and, if possible, the stroke survivor.

"I felt totally left out," a seventy-three-year-old stroke survivor complained: "My children talked with the doctor and social worker about what was 'best' for me. No one asked what *I* thought was best. Eventually they came to the same conclusion I had, that I would be most comfortable going back to my own home with someone coming in for a few hours each day to help me. But it hurt me terribly that they all acted as though I weren't there, that I didn't matter anymore. I still feel angry."

Sometimes, of course, you can't let your loved one decide. He or she may underestimate the type and amount of help that is needed. You may be overstretched with other responsibilities and be unable to spend much additional time with nursing duties or driving the patient to the grocery store, doctor, and other appointments. It may be that no one is home during the day at your house and the patient wouldn't be safe alone.

"My eighty-five-year-old father wanted to go back home after his stroke," said a middle-aged daughter. "He wanted Mother to care for him. But my mother also was in poor health. Dad had trouble walking, controlling his bladder and bowels, and he got confused. We often found him staggering down the sidewalk, wandering into traffic as though it weren't there. He lost his temper easily and threw things. Mother was in her eighties, too. She just couldn't cope with being a nurse anymore. I travel on business, so I'm gone frequently. Although we tried to bring Dad into the discussions, he stubbornly insisted that he wanted to go home and at once. He couldn't accept his or our limitations. We finally had to make the decision to put him in a nursing home. It was the only solution that worked for us, but far from a satisfying one. Even though he comes home on weekends, it's been sad and frustrating for all of us."

Leaving the Hospital

Often it comes as a shock to patient and family alike when the doctor says it's about time for the patient to be released from the hospital.

"I was pleased," said a forty-five-year-old man, "because it meant my father was better. But the social worker just announced to us one day that Dad would be leaving the hospital in the next few days. No one asked what he'd be going back to. I felt like a baby bird suddenly thrown out of the nest without any idea of what to do next. Nobody had prepared me for what was ahead for us.

"My father had lived alone in a small apartment not far from my family since my mother's death. He couldn't move in with us because we had a two-story house. Since the stroke he could barely walk. He'd never manage the stairs. My wife works all day and our kids are in day care. Who would take care of him?"

Another family shared the mixed feelings of delight that their mother was well enough to go home and fear of how they'd care for her.

"She can't feed herself or do any of her personal care," cried one of the daughters. "I can't lift her. I feel totally useless. I work full-time with irregular hours. How am I going to be able to look after her?"

"We'll never put her in a nursing home," the other daughter exclaimed. "Never. We'll find a way somehow." She paused. "It was so much easier having her here at the hospital. We knew she was getting proper care. We didn't worry so much. Now . . ." She looked away, her eyes filling with tears.

These mixed feelings are common. You're pleased, naturally, that your family member has recovered enough to be able to leave the hospital. But suddenly the realization that your life has changed, that the responsibility is now yours, is overwhelming.

"People don't realize just how short a time their loved one will spend in the acute care hospital," says Robert J.

Hartke, senior psychologist at the Rehabilitation Institute of Chicago. "It used to be much longer, and the family had time to adjust to what had happened. Now they don't have time to integrate emotionally. The patient is released before that process happens. It takes a tremendous amount of time to understand what has happened—how a stroke that occurs in seconds or minutes will affect everyone else in the family from now on. The family needs time to develop an adaptation. It truly is a process. There's no magic. It takes time, sometimes as much as six months, for natural recovery to meet adaptation."

But you don't have that time. Once the patient is stabilized, he or she soon will be released from the acute care facility. There are a great many decisions—important decisions—to be made, and you may feel unequal to the task. It's frightening to feel so responsible for another person, especially for an adult. Also, you don't have the luxury of taking months to make a decision as you might if it was just preparing for gradual aging and the need for more security and care for a parent. But although you may be more pressed for time when dealing with a stroke, you don't have to make these decisions alone. In addition to other family members, there are professionals—doctors, social workers, family counselors, religious leaders—who can help you, too.

It's important to get input from these professionals before making your decision. They know the various options along with the specific pros and cons of each. They're trained to help and usually can be most helpful, if you allow them to.

It's also a good idea to have these professionals intercede when the family members can't seem to make any definite conclusions because of power pulls or just plain shock and fatigue. The professional advisers don't come laden with the emotional baggage that families seem to come with or concerns about Mama giving the antique jewelry to Mary if she stays with her or making John Jr. do his share. They can cut through all those fears and jealousies, some of which have surprisingly resurfaced from childhood, to help determine what really is best for Mama, as well as the rest of the family.

The social worker, along with the nursing staff, works with a family to formulate plans for "what happens next." According to Dr. Hartke, "People's ingenuity is surprising. We give the ideal; people piece it together." Many families organize an informal network of assistance, blending neighbors and relatives with the availability of various social services. "The family needs to become empowered," Hartke stressed. "They need to take control of their lives and the life of their stroke survivor and become educated consumers of services."

Don't visualize the hospital or rehabilitation unit's social worker as Hollywood's stereotyped version of the social worker: a college graduate with a few sociology courses and a great deal of enthusiasm and determination who works with the poor, homeless, and the needy.

Hospital clinical social workers are specifically trained at a master's degree level to understand the patient's and family's psychological and sociological needs after a stroke. They also are well versed in their particular community's resources and can advise you on cost, type, and availability of caregiving facilities such as nursing homes, respite care, and adult day care centers; tell you how to tap into services such as Meals on Wheels, Visiting Nurse Association, and Family Services; and suggest where to get nursing aids such as folding wheelchairs, walkers, and the like.

The social worker knows the way through much of today's governmental red tape maze and can give you a great deal of guidance and support. Don't try to reinvent the wheel and do everything yourself. The hospital or rehabilitation center specifically hires its social workers to help you. Be patient, however, if you can't get immediate attention. Unfortunately, as with many of the caregiving professions, most of these dedicated men and women are seriously overworked (and underpaid).

Share in the Decision-Making Process

Many families report that their family member's stroke brought the family closer together, at least for a while. Even in families where relationships had been strained, the individuals were able to pull together while the crisis existed. Unfortunately, in many cases, once the stroke survivor seems out of danger and the doctors begin talking of releasing the patient, the fear of added responsibility melts the glue that previously united the family.

"Usually there are one or two family members that 'take over,' " said Dr. Peter Dunne, a Tampa neurologist. "They're usually the ones who make the decisions, although I suggest that everyone get involved for mutual support and so no one can complain later. If the patient is alert, it's also important to bring him or her into the decision-making process as much as possible."

Often it is possible to make temporary plans that are subject to change if and when the patient's condition improves. For example, a particular stroke survivor might be best cared for at a nursing home facility until swallowing difficulties improve or someone at home recovers from a short illness or surgery. He might stay with a relative until the proper helpers can be located to allow him to return to his own home. The patient's fears may be eased if he feels a particular situation is only temporary. Similarly, a family member may be more willing to accept a particular plan of action if he feels it isn't written in stone.

Usually, however, it's impossible to make everyone happy with all the decisions. Strokes do change the lives of an entire family, altering the structure of a family, requiring additional time and financial commitments, and redefining relationships. If everyone understands that up-front, there should be fewer misunderstandings later.

Why "Going Home" Is an Emotional Visit

Why is it so difficult, this homecoming? Probably because it conjures up all the emotions. You're happy that your family member is leaving the hospital, nervous that you won't know how to care for him, angry that you've been placed in this difficult position, frightened that he might have another stroke, and exhausted from lack of sleep and the tension and strain you've been under.

On top of these emotions, you may be overloaded with advice from well-meaning friends that leaves you so confused, you don't remember what it was the doctor told you to do and not to do. You have a handful of prescriptions that must be filled, appointments with therapists at conflicting times and/or days of the weeks, and faulty plumbing at home. Mix all that in with a few of your own personal and business responsibilities and you'll understand why you feel like crawling into the nearest cave and hiding.

You're not the only person to feel that way. It doesn't mean you're a poor excuse for a relative or that you really don't care. It means you're human and you're scared. We all are. Welcome to the club.

=== 4 ===

The Rehabilitation Center

Formerly, stroke patients remained in the acute care facility long enough so that a great deal of rehabilitation was done there. Now, however, with Medicare and other insurance providers dictating (and minimizing) the length of hospital stays, stroke survivors leave the acute care facility and receive therapy either at home or at a rehabilitation center, a facility (either part of a hospital or a free-standing unit) where both in- and outpatient therapy takes place. The purpose of this therapy is to discover and restore as much of the stroke survivor's former abilities as possible and to teach new methods for performing various tasks in order for the person to become more independent.

Rehabilitation, of course, means different things for different people. For a secretary, it might mean being able to return to her office, being functional enough to operate numerous complex office machines, take dictation, type, handle phone calls, and so on. For a nonworking homemaker, it might mean being able to get around in a wheelchair or walker, to continue to care for her home, her children, handle cooking chores, and the like. Just as every stroke is unique, the goals of rehabilitation are different for each person and his or her circumstances. The possibility of reaching these goals is hard to predict, as they depend on many things, including the stroke patient's age, motivation, other illnesses or disabilities, frustration tolerance level, mental awareness, sensory deficits, problems with incontinence, quality and amount of family support, and, generally, the extent of damage created by the stroke. How a person reacted to difficult situations in the past may also influence the degree of success in rehabilitation efforts.

What Do Rehabilitation Centers Do?

Although stroke rehabilitation centers differ depending on facilities and staffing, most of them offer a variety of services:

- neuropsychological testing
- physical therapy
- speech therapy
- dysphagia therapy
- occupational therapy
- social services
- recreation therapy
- patient and family education
- patient and family counseling
- vocational counseling
- medical care as needed

Usually the patient is referred to the rehabilitation center when the physician feels the facility's services can be of help to the stroke survivor. Some doctors, however, express doubts about the need for therapy at all, especially if the patient is elderly. Sadly, because of this attitude, many stroke survivors in their later years are denied the chance to relearn skills that could have made their remaining years more fulfilling.

Also, some families don't know that rehabilitation therapy exists. If the physician doesn't think rehabilitation is appropriate, these families take the patient home and make the best of the situation, not realizing that there might have been more potential improvement had therapy been undertaken. This is not to say that therapy can make your family member just like he was before the stroke. Therapy works miracles, but only within a reality framework.

Therapy can, however, improve most deficits in some way, not only training the stroke survivor for as much independence as is possible, but also helping the family cope by teaching them how to treat incontinence and bowel problems; showing ways of maintaining proper skin care to prevent bedsores; instructing them on ways to move the patient without injuring themselves; and showing ways in which they can work with the patient who has difficulty swallowing and, therefore, eating.

Some major rehabilitation facilities, such as the Rehabilitation Institute of Chicago, offer special driver's training programs, where the stroke patient can "drive" in a car simulator, testing himself in traffic conditions and other situations for reaction time without running the risk of danger to himself or others. If the instructor feels that it is safe for the patient to return to driving, he works with him before allowing the patient to take the driving test. However, according to Kate Brennan, a dedicated and enthusiastic nurse therapist at the Rehabilitation Institute of Chicago: "Many stroke patients do not return to driving. Their responses tend to slow down after a stroke."

Many rehabilitation centers have model apartments, where the family moves in with the patient to practice "self-care" under the watchful eye of a therapist, who oversees their living habits and makes suggestions on how best to deal with the stroke survivor and his particular problems.

Rehabilitation specialists also teach a family how to adapt their home to the stroke survivor's needs, demonstrate cooking techniques for the physically impaired patient, and suggest leisure activities, both on a personal and community level. Many also offer mock job interviews for patients returning to the labor market and help with job placement.

Who Goes to a Rehabilitation Center?

If there is a rehabilitation facility near you, ask the doctor if that is a consideration for your family member. If he says "no," press it and ask why. If you have any doubts or desire a second opinion, contact your nearest rehabilitation center and ask them for a consultation and evaluation. It could make a difference in the stroke survivor's quality of life. It could also improve your knowledge and ability to care for your family member. Appendix A offers a partial listing of rehabilitation units and free-standing centers that have reported having organized inpatient and/or outpatient stroke programs.

I've personally visited three rehab centers and find that they are amazing places. I've not only come away uplifted and encouraged by all that's positive in mankind, but it's also helped keep my own priorities straight. Many rehabilitation centers also house patients with orthopedic problems and spinal cord injuries. A trip in the elevator may put you face to face with a paraplegic pushing himself in his wheelchair, a crippled child on crutches, and a stroke survivor on his way to occupational therapy. There is a wonderful spirit of camaraderie among patients and staff alike.

New patients are evaluated by the stroke team to determine their specific needs and are encouraged to do as much for themselves as possible. They are taught ADL (activities of daily living) which include how to dress and feed themselves, care for personal hygiene, and other hand skills. They learn to perfect the important skill of transfer (getting from the wheelchair to the bath, bed, or car and back again) and to otherwise care for themselves. There is a great deal of individual attention, with programs personalized to each patient's particular needs.

You and other family members are welcomed and actually encouraged to observe therapy sessions so you know how to help when the stroke survivor returns home. These professionals understand that you and the other members of your family need both educational and emotional support in order to cope with the days ahead. Often the rehabilitation staff meets with the family to discuss specific issues and may offer special seminars for families of stroke survivors.

Most rehabilitation centers treat patients on both an inpatient and an outpatient basis. Those who are inpatients receive a daily schedule of activities and therapy sessions and, if able, are encouraged to assume the responsibility of getting to their class by themselves. Meals are usually served in a large communal dining room.

I expected to be depressed by my visits to rehabilitation centers. Instead I felt as though I were in a unique college dorm with organized confusion, gentle bantering among the inhabitants, and even some hand-holding as romance blossomed. Everyone seemed to know where he or she was going. No one was too busy to hold a door, answer a question, or retrieve a baseball cap when it toppled off its owner. I felt pride for the dedicated and tireless staff as well as for the patients, whose determination was obvious. I wondered, could *I* face the same difficulties and keep trying?

"I hadn't wanted to go to a rehab center. I just wanted to go hide in a corner," a fifty-year-old stroke patient confessed. "But to my surprise, it made me feel better to see how much more I could do than some of the other stroke survivors. Having to learn to feed myself with my left hand didn't seem so terrible when I saw how bad off some of the others were. Those who had learned the skills they needed to adapt to their particular problem encouraged me to push myself."

Stroke Clubs

Many rehabilitation centers also sponsor stroke clubs, where stroke survivors and their families meet on a regular basis to share and solve problems and to make new friends. A psychologist or social worker usually helps to conduct the meetings to make sure they remain beneficial to all the members.

A stroke club offers you a chance to talk to others who

are in your shoes. Somehow it's usually comforting to know you aren't alone with a problem and that others have faced and overcome similar situations. You may get some good ideas on how to handle a particular problem; you may just get a reassuring pat from a person who is as concerned, tired, and frustrated as you. Do remember, however, that every stroke is different. Don't compare your stroke patient with others who appear to have suffered similar strokes. Stroke clubs are for comfort and companionship, not competition.

Stroke clubs also serve another important function. They give the stroke survivor an additional opportunity for social contact. Unfortunately, the stroke patient's former social life—and yours, too—may slow down a little after he gets out of the hospital. Invitations stop coming. People don't mean to be cruel; they just don't know how to handle someone who has trouble speaking or walking. "Might make Joe feel uncomfortable if we invite him to the dance," they rationalize, not realizing that you and Joe have sat home staring at each other for weeks now, and an outing and chance to dress up—even if Joe can't dance anymore—would be a marvelous change of pace. The stroke club offers that outing. Don't feel self-conscious. Everyone there is in the same boat. You've nothing to lose. Try it.

If there isn't a stroke club in your area, contact one of your hospitals or your local chapter of the American Heart Association or the National Easter Seal Society. If you and other families of stroke survivors are interested in organizing a stroke club yourselves, contact the National Easter Seal Society and ask for their detailed publication entitled *Organizing a Stroke Club*. It offers excellent suggestions for getting a club started, how to get members, activities, program ideas, and other suggestions. You can send for it by writing them at:

The National Easter Seal Society
70 East Lake Street
Chicago, Illinois 60601
(312) 853-9690

Send a check or money order for $1.20, made out to the National Easter Seal Society.

The Courage Stroke Network also has information on how to form a stroke club. You can write them at

Courage Stroke Network
Courage Center
3915 Golden Valley Road
Golden Valley, Minnesota 55422
(612) 588-0811

Weaning the Patient from the Rehabilitation Center

Many families of stroke survivors complain that once the patient gets home, he "seems different" from the way he was in the rehabilitation center.

"He seemed comfortable there," said the sister of a forty-year-old stroke survivor. "He joked with the nurses and the other patients. Now he's irritable and depressed. There, he did everything they asked him to. I can't even get him to lift a finger. What happened?"

To find out, I questioned a few people who had spent two weeks or more in a rehabilitation center. Their answers surprised me:

1. They *did* feel more comfortable in the rehabilitation center. They knew the staff was professional and well trained; at home, their family seemed ill at ease and uncertain how to deal with them.

2. At the rehabilitation center, all the patients were there to overcome a problem. People had speech deficits, were paralyzed on one side, had trouble swallowing, and so on. At home, they were the only "odd" ones. They felt more conspicuous. Worse, they found it harder to practice what they had learned because they were the only ones doing it. Even with the most willing relative, they felt they were a burden and that they needed to "hurry" with their lesson.

3. The stress, of course, made their practice sessions less successful than they had been in the rehabilitation center. They became less functional than they had been at the rehab center, and that made them feel depressed and withdrawn.

4. Coming home also meant adjusting to yet another change. People who have had strokes don't adapt well to changing environments. So much has changed in their lives that they take comfort in familiarity. It wasn't that they didn't like being home as much as it meant readjusting to yet another space, different routines, different sounds, and different faces.

What can the family do? How can they wean the stroke survivor from the comforting cocoon of the rehabilitation center and back into the world, the unprotected world of reality?

1. Don't take it personally.

That's easier said than done, of course. Here you have given up much of your valuable time and energies to help care for your family member, and like Rodney Dangerfield, you get no respect.

2. Discuss your feelings with the stroke patient.

Tell him that you realize you're just learning how to help him, but that you need his help and cooperation, just as he needs yours. This discussion becomes a difficult, if not impossible, task if he has receptive communication problems and doesn't understand what you're saying. He may just look at you—which can be even more frustrating. You can try to pantomime the message—pointing to you, then him, then clasping hands—but it may be too vague a point to get across.

3. Try to keep things orderly.

Stroke patients need familiarity to keep some sense of order in their lives. A magazine on the couch, a dirty glass on the table, can be very frustrating. If they're living with you, it may be difficult to keep a tidy house along with everything else you have to do. It may be especially hard if you have small children or pets as well.

Establish a routine as much as possible, so the person knows when he is to bathe (or be bathed), when you work with him on speech (or the therapist comes or he goes to clinic), and when mealtimes are. You might draw a picture of a clock to show the time or have a large calendar with the therapy dates marked in red. If he doesn't understand the visual signs, try sound cues or even appeal to the sense of touch by bringing out a furry lap robe or a velvet pillow when it's time for speech therapy. It takes trial and error and a lot of time and patience.

4. Ask for help.

Have the speech therapist explain to you again exactly what you're supposed to do with the words list; let the physical therapist show you how to help with the exercises. If you're doing something even a little bit differently from the way it was done by one of the patient's therapists, he may find it "out of order" and rebel. Contact the Visiting Nurses Association or the American Red Cross and ask for a demonstration on bathing, feeding, and dressing techniques for patients (or anything else you're having trouble with). Remember that the professionals have been trained to do these tasks and they do it every day with many patients. You're a novice, but you can be a capable one.

5. Act confident.

This may take some acting, at first, but if you try, you may convince yourself as well as the patient that you do know what you're doing. As you become more self-assured, your family member will begin to relax and let you help. He'll also start to enjoy the benefits of being back in his own surroundings.

Rehabilitation doesn't end when your family member leaves the rehab center and goes home or moves in with you. Many experts say that additional improvement can continue for six months after the stroke and often for as much as a year or two more. It's a continuing process, in which you and the patient strive continually not for perfection, but for the best use of those abilities that are still functional, so that the stroke survivor can enjoy life and living as much as is possible.

5

When the Stroke Survivor Goes Home

WHEN THEY'RE ALONE

At first it sounds wonderful that the stroke survivor has recovered enough to be able to return home. Certainly familiar surroundings are best. But when the patient lives alone, you suddenly are filled with myriad concerns.

Questions to Think About

- Will she be safe (able to handle stairs, bathe, leave in case of an emergency)?
- What if she falls?
- Can she fix a simple meal without danger?
- Will she bother to eat?
- Can she handle her medication needs?
- Is she able to call for help in case of illness or danger? Use the phone? Push a button?
- Will she become depressed?
- Do I feel comfortable with this decision?
- Can I accept the fact that my loved one could suffer another stroke and I wouldn't be there, that it is a risk we're both willing to take because life is full of risks?

These were just a few of the questions that filled our minds when we were told that our mother would soon be released from the hospital. We were assured that her speech therapy could be continued at home. She didn't require physical therapy. Although she could have gone to our community's fine rehabilitation center, she really didn't require many of their services. Their beds were badly needed by people with more severe residual effects from their strokes. Also, she wanted to go home. And we wanted her at home, too, but we had doubts—severe doubts—about her being alone in her condo.

In retrospect, the issue we couldn't face was that we couldn't bear for her to be alone in case "something" happened (another stroke or other illness) without us there. It was guilt, plain and clear. We were her children. We should take care of her. We wanted to, and it was our duty. But my sister lived out of town, my brother and I worked and had families. We couldn't be with her all the time. So we decided to find someone who could.

Is a "Live-in" the Answer?

At first, in order to protect her and free us from guilt, we decided that Mother needed to have a "live-in"—not a nurse, we assured her, but a companion.

We totally ignored the fact that our mother was a fairly solitary person. She always enjoyed her own company and some "quiet time." Over the three and a half years that our father had been in a nursing home, Mother had adjusted reasonably well to being alone. She read, napped, and watched television. Her activities consisted primarily of attending to business matters a few days a week, playing mah-jongg and lunching with friends, doing the grocery shopping, and going to the beauty parlor. She went to an occasional movie and enjoyed theater at our performing arts center. But she was not a gadabout; she did not require constant chatter or continuous company.

Nevertheless, feeling most righteous that we were "doing the right thing for mother," we contacted social service agencies, the Visiting Nurse Association, and private nursing agencies. Live-in companions, we discovered, were difficult to find.

Our mother required no special nursing. She could bathe, dress, feed, and amuse herself. Her reading ability, never affected greatly by the stroke, quickly returned to the point where she could read and understand magazine articles again. Soon she would be back to enjoying full-length novels as she had before. The only help she really required was someone to answer the phone (since she couldn't speak), cook her meals, and drive her wherever she wanted to go.

Everyone's needs are different. If your family member has additional disabilities from the stroke, you may need someone to help with bathing, personal grooming, and dressing as well as giving medications. Obviously a bedridden stroke survivor has far different needs from someone who only requires help with cooking or driving.

Live-in Wish List

Before beginning your search, complete the following **live-in wish list.** This will help you to visualize what you want—and help you decide what concessions you are willing to make, if necessary.

Live-in Wish List ·

Requirements	A "Must"	Prefer	Not important
24-hour duty:			
Man:			
Woman:			
Financial requirements:			
Nonsmoker:			
Driver's license:			
Local references:			
Experience w/stroke patients:			

Willingness
to help
w/ therapy:

Cooking ability:

Nursing training:

Bilingual:

Religious
preference:

Housework:

Light housework:

Ironing:

Sense of humor:

Understanding na-
ture:

Cost for a Live-In

Cost for such twenty-four-hour live-in service varies widely, depending on whether or not the person has nursing training (which ranges from a few classes taken by a home health aide to a registered nurse), whether you hire through an agency or directly, and what you need the person to do. I received quotes from as low as minimum wage to $50 an hour. You also need to make backup provisions for when the caregiver has time off, is ill, or is on vacation.

Housing the Live-In

Is there adequate space for a live-in helper? Many stroke survivors live in smaller apartments or condominiums. Although it's possible to find someone willing to sleep on a couch in the living room, most people who take a live-in job expect to have their own room, and preferably, a private bathroom.

Who Wants the Live-In?

Discuss this with the other family members up-front. Who really wants live-in help? Does the patient really want someone to live in, or do the rest of you think it's a good idea so *you* won't have to worry? Unless the patient is totally bed-ridden and needs complete care, your best intentions may be sabotaged if the stroke survivor resents having someone around all the time. Although some people enjoy constant companionship, far more resent the intrusion into their former privacy. Even if the helper has her own suite, the stroke survivor may feel a loss of independence. Discuss this issue before you waste valuable time and energy trying to find someone to live in.

If you're lucky, you'll find the right person quickly and they'll stay as long as they're needed. Most of us, however, make compromises on what we wanted originally and spend almost as much time looking for help as we would have by doing it all ourselves.

Expect a high turnover. It's hard to find people willing to move into someone else's home on a full-time basis.

"We've gone through twenty-five live-in home health aides," a middle-aged woman said sadly. "My father found fault with every one of them—this one 'laughed funny,' that one wouldn't let him watch the TV show he wanted, another smoked, even though we requested someone who didn't. The ones he didn't dislike eventually quit anyway because he was so demanding. One quit *before* she was due to start because he had been so rude to her at the interview."

Almost every family member interviewed for this book had similar stories. As difficult as it was for those who lived in the same town with their ailing parent, sibling, or other relative, it was an impossible situation for those who lived in another community. Many gave up trying to find "good help" and either took the stroke survivor into their home or found space in a nursing home or other institutional housing.

Using the Split-Shift

Some families get around the difficulty in finding a live-in helper by arranging for help on a split-shift basis. This can be done through an agency or by using friends, family members, and nonprofessionals recommended by others.

Advantages of the Split-Shift Arrangement

New faces at each shift provide more interest and stimulation for the patient.

Easier to cope with someone less than "perfect" when you know it's only for a shift, rather than twenty-four hours.

Makes replacement easier.

The people on the different shifts often switch around to cover for each other, which relieves you of one more responsibility.

Can arrange more skilled help during the hours needed— for bathing, therapy, tube feedings, and so on, and use less expensive help during the night when a responsible person is needed only in case of emergency.

Disadvantages of the Split-Shift Arrangement

More expensive through a professional agency than a live-in.

The "coming and going" may confuse a stroke patient, who is already easily distracted.

More people for you to interview, check on, make payment arrangements with, and the like.

Over time, petty jealousies and resentments may arise, often aided by the stroke patient, who, like a child, quickly learns to play one caregiver against another.

Part-Time Helper

For the person with slight disabilities, the part-time helper may be the best answer. It gives the stroke survivor who is used to living alone the privacy he or she needs yet relieves you and other family members from constant worry and/or having to dash over ten times a day.

Advantages of the Part-Time Helper

Cheaper than other arrangements because you only have to pay for the time she is there.

You can specify exact needs, such as help with bathing, giving medications, assisting with physical therapy exercises, and so forth.

It's usually easier to find someone for a few hours a day than for longer stretches.

The stroke patient feels more independent.

More flexibility with changing hours.

Disadvantages of the Part-Time Helper

Stroke survivor is alone much of the day.

Speech may regress without someone there to talk to and be stimulated by.

Part-time worker may take job less seriously.

Helper may not be able to complete all tasks in allotted time.

You may have more responsibilities, such as cooking, cleaning, laundry, and so on.

Good help *is* available in most communities. Unfortunately it is difficult to find, difficult to keep, and limited in number. Luckily most stroke survivors don't require totally skilled nursing such as one gets with registered nurses or licensed practical nurses. The needs vary from person to person, of course, but often what's required is "an honest, dependable, and caring person to cook, do light housework, and take the stroke survivor to appointments and shopping." The schedule may vary from a few hours each day to all day with someone else sleeping in at night. Some people, who have the space, prefer to have the same person living in.

How Do You Find Helpers?

There are a variety of ways to find helpers.

Visiting Nurse Association

Check your phone book or ask your hospital social worker. If yours is not one of the five hundred communities where VNA is located, write

The Visiting Nurse Association of America
3801 E. Florida Ave., Suite 806
Denver, Colorado 80210
Phone: 1-800-426-2547

Your Religious Social Services Organization

Most religious organizations have lists of men and women who care for the sick, along with lists of services within your particular community. Contact your minister, rabbi, or priest.

Your Community's Family Services Program

Contact United Way in your area or check the white pages of your phone book under Family Services or Social Service Agencies.

Commercial Nursing Agencies

The for-profit business world has caught on to the fact that home health care is a growing industry. Scores of new health care agencies appear on the scene each year. Some, like Kelly Assisted Living and Upjohn Healthcare Services, are national companies, providing customized services including cooking, dressing, running errands, and companionship for $8 or $9 an hour. Other home health agencies are local organizations, privately owned or branches of local hospitals, which also want a piece of the long-term home health care pie.

If you seek help through an agency, be sure that its

employees are prescreened, fully bonded, insured, and licensed by your particular state.

An advantage of working with an agency is that you can begin with a registered nurse, if necessary, and then cut back to home health aides through the same agency, when your relative is able to have less skilled nursing. They also can provide emergency backups.

Don't assume, however, that because someone has been screened and hired through an agency, he or she will be perfect. When my mother fell and broke her ankle, the home health aide who was with her not only didn't bother to take her to a doctor or contact me, she also didn't bother to relay that information to her supervisors, which we had been assured was the policy.

Word of Mouth

As you might expect, finding help through the recommendation of a friend still seems to be one of the best ways to find a companion or part-time assistance for your family member.

Often it is someone without special training, either an older woman who is working to supplement her income or someone who just enjoys working with older people or being needed.

You do need to check references very carefully, however. We were given the name of someone "who was just wonderful with Mrs. Cohen." When we checked with the late Mrs. Cohen's daughter, however, we found that she had been ready to fire this "wonderful lady" because she had come by early to take her mother for a ride and overheard the companion tormenting her mother. The old lady had been afraid of more mistreatment if she told her daughter, so she had remained silent. Only her mother's death prevented the daughter from firing the companion, and her honesty kept us from hiring her.

College Student

Notwithstanding what you may read in the papers, there are a great many reliable students working their way through school who may be interested in working a few hours each day or sleeping at your family member's home, trading room and board for helping to care for a stroke survivor. A student nurse is also a possibility if you live near a nursing school.

Cost varies for these different types of service. Although it may be cheaper to use someone recommended to you by a friend, the home aides sent from recognized agencies usually have had some medical or first-aid training, often prescribed by state or local requirements. Be sure you know what type of help you really need before beginning your search.

How to Interview

Regardless of who you get or how great the recommendations are, interview the candidate in person and, if possible, have the stroke survivor there as well. Even if your family member can't speak, you should be able to see some interplay going on between them. Watch closely for subtle clues through body language telling you how the patient feels about the prospective helper.

Have a list of prepared questions for your interviewee and jot down notes to remind you of the answers. Don't be so busy asking questions, however, that you fail to listen to what is being said as well as how. Before ending the interview, give applicants time to ask questions of their own.

Your list of questions should include the following:

1. The person I'm looking for should have the following qualifications: (name them). Do you think you qualify, and if so, why?
2. Why do you want this job?
3. What experience do you have working with stroke

patients? What about people who have difficulty with their speech?

4. Do you have any driving violations? If so, what are they for?
5. Do you smoke?
6. What are your drinking habits?
7. What medications do you take?
8. What work are you doing now?
9. What are your other responsibilities?
10. What concerns do you have about this job?
11. Tell me about yourself—health, hobbies, personality, temperament . . .

Describe the hours you want filled and what you plan to pay. Get their reaction. If you're interviewing for a live-in person, show them or describe where they'll be living. Ask if that is satisfactory. They may want to bring their own TV, clock radio, and so on, so say whether or not you'll feel comfortable with them settling in with their own possessions.

Finally, check ahead of time to see if the stroke patient has any preference as to whether or not the person wears a uniform. Some people want their help to be dressed like a nurse, while others may resent the suggestion that they are sick and prefer the helper to dress like a companion. Discuss your decision with the interviewee to get her reaction. Some helpers prefer wearing a uniform to show that they are "professional." Others may feel it is demeaning.

Before ending the interview, ask the person if she has any questions. Say that you'll be checking references and will get back in touch as soon as you have made a decision.

You might also consider giving them a form to complete.

Caregiver/Helper Application Form

Date: ___ / ___ / ___

Name: _____
         (first)   (middle)   (last)

What do you prefer being called?_____

Address: _____
         (street)   (city)   (state)   (zip)

Phone Number: (   ) _____
                (area code)

Social Security number: _____-____-_____

Education:
   High School: _____graduated? yes ____no ____
   College: (please name) _____

   Any additional training: _____

Health Care experience: (please specify amount of time)

_____

_____

References:
Name	Address	Phone Number	Relationship (former employee, friend, minister)
1)			
2)			
3)			

Do you drive? yes ____ no ____
   Have you had any violations in the past five years (please list any on back of page)?

This will give you, in writing, the applicant's name, address, phone number, Social Security number, and names of references and will also show you how well the person writes, understands, and answers questions, and follows instructions.

As soon as the interviewee leaves, write down your immediate impressions. If you're interviewing a great many people, you may forget who had the shifty eyes and who made your mother smile.

Always take the time and have the courtesy to call everyone back once you have made a decision. It's important to keep your options open. You may need your second choice if your first choice changes *her* mind.

Some patients do well with a "take charge" type of person, who decides when they'll go shopping or out for a drive. Others may resent what they perceive as bossiness and loss of independence. If your family member is not used to having someone around, expect some complaints.

Expect some disappointments, too. Some people who almost seem too good to be true, aren't. One daughter popped in unexpectedly to see her mother, only to overhear the helper threatening to leave the mother alone in the house if she didn't eat the unappetizing mess that was in front of her.

I was awakened from a deep sleep at three A.M. by the well-recommended helper I had carefully interviewed and just hired that day to stay with my mother, who said she was leaving immediately because she was bored and felt "penned up."

A friend found her father's aide drunk and sound asleep in front of the television set while her father wept from fear and hunger in his soiled bed. She angrily called the person who had recommended the aide. He admitted he knew the aide had a drinking problem but hadn't wanted to hurt her chances of getting a job.

Fortunately these are exceptions. Although many of those interviewed said they weren't 100 percent satisfied with the person they had hired for their family member, most admitted that the care was good and that the stroke patient seemed comfortable and reasonably happy most of the time.

How Can You Be Sure?

You can't, but you can drop in often without calling first. If you live out of town, ask a friend to check for you. Here are a few things to look for:

- **Is the patient out of bed, if possible?**
- **Is the patient clean?**
- **If the patient is a man, is he freshly shaven? If a woman, is she well groomed?**

This is not petty. How a person—especially one who has suffered so many personal losses from a stroke—looks has a great deal to do with a good self-image and how he or she feels and reacts. Pride in one's appearance plays an important part in forestalling depression.

- **Is the patient dressed or still in a bathrobe?**
- **Does there seem to be a good rapport between the stroke survivor and the caregiver?**

Even if your family member can't speak, you can read the body language. Does she seem afraid or resentful of the caregiver, or is there gentle joking between them?

- **Is the home or apartment kept clean and litter free?**
- **Are there dirty dishes sitting around?**
- **Is there dried-up or spoiled food in the refrigerator?**
- **What kind of food is being prepared?**

Is it canned? Junk food? Is it appropriate for specific dietary needs? Many stroke survivors must stay on low-cholesterol diets. Be sure that the aide understands these requirements and doesn't whip up high-cholesterol grilled-cheese sandwiches and bacon and fried eggs because they're easy to prepare.

There are a number of other decisions you need to make in relation to having someone else in the house with your family member.

• **How do you handle the grocery money?**

Do you leave cash? If so, how will it be accounted for? If there's a charge account with the grocer, how can you make sure that everything purchased is for your family member?

• **What about personal effects?**

If your loved one is bedridden or seriously impaired, you might want to collect the jewelry and other valuables rather than leave them sitting out offering temptation. Many times these things disappear, not because of the helper, but through the patient's actions. Stroke patients who are confused may throw things into the wastebasket or down a garbage chute. If your grandfather's watch and fob is special to you or you want to pass your mother's ring down to your own daughter, take them for safekeeping.

• **What contingency plans do you have if the aide quits or becomes ill?**

• **What about days off?**

These matters are handled by the respective agencies when you hire helpers from them. When you do your own hiring, you need to make backup plans before they're needed.

• **How will you handle medical needs?**

Be sure the helper knows what medicine is to be given, when, and how. You might want to use the chart in Illustration E so that you have a permanent record.

- Leave emergency phone numbers where you and other family members can be reached.
- Be sure the doctor's phone number is in plain sight.
- If there is more than one hospital in your community, list the name of your preference.
- Write down the patient's address and apartment number (if any) so that someone calling for help knows it.
- List the names of people who may be calling so the helper can tell the patient, even if she can't speak to them.

One far-thinking daughter gave a Rolodex to her mother's helper. Every friend and family member was listed with clues as to who they were and how they were related, such as "Janet Davis, David's youngest daughter. Mother's granddaughter." That way, when Janet called to ask about her grandmother, the aide was able to know the relationship and importance of who had called.

Obviously the best situation is when the stroke survivor can return home with a minimum of change and, with a little help, continue to live as before. If this doesn't work, or if you and/or the patient are afraid to have her living alone, even with some help, then you may decide to have her move in with you.

WHEN THEY'RE HOME, BUT NOT ALONE

But what if the stroke survivor comes home, not to an empty apartment or house, but back into the midst of an active family or, as is often the case, an aging spouse who suffers from his or her own other age-related ailments and really isn't strong enough to be a caregiver? Although these two situations can benefit from some of the suggestions mentioned early in this chapter, they also bring with them other problems to be understood and solved, if possible.

Illustration E

Medical Reminder Chart

Note: Avoid missing any dose of medication.
Do not stop taking medication without doctor's permission.

Format #1: For patient staying alone or with part-time helper
(Mark pill bottles with colored felt-tip pen or colored label)

7AM	8AM	10AM	11AM	12N	2PM	3PM	4PM	5PM	6PM	8PM
Drink 8 oz. water	Breakfast	Drink 10 oz. water	Call Brian	Eat lunch	Drink 10 oz. fluids	Call Brian	Drink 10 oz. fluids	Eat dinner	Drink fluids	Drink fluids
Dilantin one pill from red bottle (200 mg.)	Tenormin one pill from blue bottle (100 mg.)		Mylanta II one tablespoon from green bottle	Drink 10 oz. fluids			Mylanta II one tablespoon from green bottle	Pancrease three capsules		Mylanta II one tablespoon from green bottle
				Paregoric one teaspoon from brown bottle				Dilantin one pill from red bottle (200 mg.)		Dilantin one pill from red bottle (200 mg.)

(adapted from chart courtesy of Rehabilitation Institute of Chicago)

Illustration E
Format #2: For family or helper regulating medication
(Keep all information in a folder or loose-leaf notebook)

MEDICATION	TIME				PURPOSE	SIDE EFFECTS/ IMPLICATIONS
	8AM	12N	5PM	9PM		
THEO-DUR 200 mg. one tablet 3 times daily.	●	●	●		Makes it easier to breathe by relaxation of smooth muscle in the airway.	• Take this medication on a regular schedule. • Take with meals. • May cause nausea, insomnia, palpitations.
TEGRETOL 200 mg. one tablet 3 times daily.	●	●	●		Used for prevention and treatment of seizures.	• May cause nausea, vomiting, fever, sore throat, skin patches.
PERI-COLACE one capsule twice daily	●		●		Used to relieve constipation.	• May cause loose stool, cramps.
VASOTEC 2.5 mg. ½ tablet twice daily	●		●		Used to treat high blood pressure.	• May cause headache, dizziness, fatigue, diarrhea.
COUMADIN 4 mg. (2 tab) on even days 2 mg. (1 tab) on odd days.				●	Blood thinner. Prevents harmful clot formation in blood vessels.	• Nosebleeds, bruising, bleeding gums, black/tar bowel movements. • Periodic lab test will be needed.

Returning to the Family

Obviously we all want our spouse or parent back where he or she belongs—within the family circle. But unless the patient has only minor residual effects from the stroke, there are bound to be some major differences, changes that affect not only the person who has suffered the stroke, but the entire family unit.

Accept the Patient as He Is

This is far easier to say than it is to carry out. Our emotions get in the way. We want the person we love back the way he was prestroke. But it's unlikely he will be. So, along with feelings of concern for his safety and morale, we have doubts about our ability to care for him and a profound sadness for what might have been.

Shortly before her stroke, my mother, an avid reader, had shown a great interest in taking a course offered by our local library that would prepare her to tutor an illiterate. She was so enthusiastic about the proposed project that I had toyed with making time to join her.

"I'll never be able to tutor now," she said resignedly six months after her stroke. Although she speaks reasonably well, she knew she wouldn't be able to function properly as a tutor. She also suffers from extreme fatigue, a common symptom for those who have suffered a stroke.

I felt sadness and regret for the loss of her dream. She would have been a great tutor; she could have made a difference to someone shut out from the world of the printed word. Life wasn't fair.

Those whose mate has had a stroke mourn too, for their lost dreams and the loss of their equal partner in life. Now they must adjust to a caregiver-patient relationship, however loving it still may be.

Will Roles Be Affected?

Roles within a marriage or family as a whole are bound to be affected by a stroke. If your husband was the main or, possibly, the only breadwinner, you'll both have to make major adjustments—financial and emotional—if he is no longer able to work to provide for the family. If he is alert and aware, the change from active businessman to home-bound keeper of the hearth may be a difficult transition. Although some men discover that they enjoy puttering around the house and become adept at cooking and caring for the home, others may feel a loss of their masculinity. Time may hang heavy for the formerly employed whose nine to five day previously was overflowing with activity.

You, on the other hand, may need to find a job. If you've worked outside the home before, you have some idea of your abilities and how to market them. For women who have never held down a paying job before, the thought of job hunting is overwhelming.

"I don't have any marketable skills," Margaret, a forty-year-old woman, confided. "I never wanted to work and never thought I'd have to. I don't know where to begin. Dave can't look after the kids. He needs someone to look after him! I'll have to hire two someones, one for him and one for my eight-year-old."

How do you begin looking for a job when you've never worked before or have been out of the job market a long time?

Professional Career Counseling
For Margaret and women like her, there are career counselors available at many Y's, Jewish Community Centers, Family Service Centers, local junior colleges, colleges, and universities, as well as at other community facilities. There are also various excellent job-hunting books on the market. One of the best, in my opinion, is *What Color Is Your Parachute?* by Richard N. Bolles.

Tell People You Need a Job
The more people you tell about your need for a job, the more likely you are to find something. Often jobs open up

and are filled without ever having been advertised. Although it's fine to read the want ads, almost every woman I know who is employed today found out about her job through word of mouth. The last company I worked for (I've been my own boss, working as a free-lance writer, for the last twenty-eight years) was recommended to me by their competition, where I had gone for an interview. They had no job openings but suggested I go to their competitor. I did, they did, and I got the job.

Most people have far more ability than they give themselves credit for. If you suddenly find yourself in the position of having to support your family, believe in yourself. You'll find work, and you'll probably soon realize not only that you are good at it, but that you like it, too! That's called confidence. You'll need it because a great deal of responsibility is now resting on your shoulders.

Encourage Your Mate

While you may be feeling heady and proud of yourself (as you should), you may not immediately notice that your spouse may be having difficulty adjusting to staying home.

Many people backslide a bit when leaving the rehabilitation center. It's often easier to force yourself to form words and take slow, painstaking steps when you're surrounded and supported by others in the same boat.

The rehabilitation center lacks the emotional content that one's own home naturally has. When the stroke survivor returns home, he is suddenly faced with his previous environment, which is now very different for him. His bedroom may have been upstairs. Now it may be out of bounds for him. There may be hobbies that no longer can be enjoyed. The entire house is filled with memories of what life used to be, dramatically underscoring what it has become.

Also, there may have been more positive reinforcement from the staff of the rehabilitation center. They can be more objective than you. Also, they are involved for an eight-hour shift, then they go home. You, on the other hand, come home from work, deal with the kids, care for your mate, possibly check on your older parents, and then have to think about the physical and speech therapy exercises. It's a lot to deal with.

"I'm ready to drop," said the wife of a stroke survivor. "I know he needs to go through these picture cards and say the words, but I'm so tired. I want to help him, really I do. But I miss our old 'How was your day?' conversations terribly. I even miss our fights. But I'm just so tired. I feel emotionally brittle."

How can you solve this? By asking for help. If your children are old enough, allow them to help Daddy or Grandpa with his lessons. Remember that they've been affected by his stroke, too. They need reinforcement that they too can help in his recovery every bit as much as he needs practice with his speech. Chapter 12 offers many suggestions of ways you can enlist help from family and friends, most of whom are eager and only waiting to be told how they can help. *Do not try to do it all by yourself.*

Expect Some Changes

In addition to the obvious changes—difficulty in speaking or walking, paralysis—there are some more subtle changes of which you should be aware.

Fatigue

Stroke survivors tend to suffer from profound fatigue. Part of it may come from depression or the extreme effort that must go into speaking and/or walking or overcoming any of the residual effects of stroke. Fatigue also has a physical basis. The body needs rest in order to heal.

1. Try to anticipate it before the person becomes exhausted.
2. Allow extra time to get ready for social engagements or medical appointments.
3. Encourage regularly scheduled naps.
4. Keep visitors' stays short.

5. Locate a "quiet spot" (den, garden, back bedroom) where the stroke survivor can get away from normal household noise and confusion. (You also can benefit from this retreat when you practice some of the relaxation techniques mentioned in chapter 12.)
6. Establish as much of a routine as possible for meals, bedtimes, home therapy, and the like.

Depression

Depression is a common side effect of stroke. It is not just an emotional response to all that has been lost. It also seems to have a very real physical component. Nevertheless, depression or a feeling of gloom can overtake a household, spreading as though it were a virus and infecting, then reinfecting, all its members. Although serious depression must be treated by a physician, there are steps a family can take to decrease mild depression.

1. Encourage the stroke survivor to join in family activities, such as going to a movie, on a picnic, or out to eat. Realize, however, that the residual effects of the stroke—problems in reception, difficulties in swallowing—may make it hard for the person to participate. He may feel self-conscious or just plain scared.
2. Assign some household task that is within his ability to complete. We all need to feel needed; stroke survivors, especially those who formerly were active and useful, suffer from loss of self-image along with their other losses. A woman unable to speak or handle numbers, and with weaknesses on one side, is still capable of watching her toddler, fixing a meal, or stuffing and stamping envelopes as her husband pays the bills.
3. Encourage friends and other family members to visit. Much depression is caused by the feeling that no one now really cares if you live or die. Visitors bring (or should bring) something new to think about, rather than focusing on what can no longer be done.

For more information on how to handle depression—both yours as well as the stroke survivor's—see chapter 10 and chapter 12.

Everything in Its Place

Routine and orderliness become paramount for the stroke survivor, perhaps because his life is in such turmoil.

"My husband is driving me crazy," an older woman confided. "He screams if I leave a towel on the bathtub. He wants it hung up almost before I've stopped using it. Yesterday he stomped into the kitchen with my drinking glass and I wasn't even through with it. Last week, when I drove us to the bank, he started punching my arm because I took a different route than he was used to."

This type of complaint kept cropping up from many family members who were frustrated with their relative's compulsive tidiness and need for specific routines. Although there's no way to minimize it, it may help to know that, as the stroke survivor becomes more comfortable with his surroundings and adjusts to his new life-style, he will become more flexible.

If, however, the person engages in anything that might harm him or others—such as the man who insisted on going to the bank in a specific way—the family member needs to say firmly, "I know you prefer going a different way. But I'm driving, and this is the way *I* go. It gets us to the bank just the same. You cannot hit my arm while I'm driving."

Any time the patient shows inappropriate behavior, such as throwing food, having a temper tantrum, or hitting, control your own temper. Don't scream back or hit. Either leave the room until you can compose yourself or count to ten, breathing deeply. Then, in the calmest voice you can muster, tell him that you can't permit this kind of behavior, that you understand his frustration, but you won't allow him to act this way.

Easy? Not at all. I brought my father an ice-cream sundae, which he usually loves. This particular day he took the cup and turned it upside-down. I tried to right it so he wouldn't lose his ice cream. Perhaps he thought I was trying to feed him (which he hates), or maybe he was just extra frustrated. He screamed at me and threw the cup with what was left of the ice cream against the wall.

I looked at the ice cream dripping down the wall. I felt like scraping it off and throwing it back at him. Instead I stood, concentrating on regulating my breathing. When I thought I could speak in a normal tone, I said, "Well, I guess you won't have any ice cream today."

He grew very quiet. As with all of us, it's important to know the parameters. I think it helped him to know I wasn't going to let him get any more out of control. I also didn't get him more ice cream.

It's Not Easy

There's nothing easy about living with someone who has had a stroke. The more extensive the residual effects, the more difficult it becomes. The person you love has changed, often into a different personality. It takes a great deal of patience, energy, understanding, and love. When you bring your family member into your home, you even compound the problems, although you may find certain aspects easier. The remaining chapters all deal with problems you will face and, hopefully, learn to overcome or at least deal with, as you learn to live with the aftereffects of stroke.

6

Bringing the Stroke Survivor into Your Home

"There's no way Mother can be alone, but I won't let her go into a nursing home. She'll have to come live with us."

Although these words have a convincing ring, too often they're said without adequate thought or depth of conversation with the rest of the family. Any addition to the household—even a baby—creates numerous changes for everyone. When you add a stroke survivor, who may have physical, emotional, and communication problems, it's bound to alter the normal balance of living considerably.

Deciding If Your Home's the Answer

There are many important factors to weigh before deciding to have your family member move into your household. It's easy to let emotion, fatigue, and true concern sway you, but try to make your decision based on reality. Discuss these considerations with your spouse and your children. You can't make it work all by yourself, even if you want to. The entire family will be involved, and their lives will be affected, so they might as well have a voice in the decision.

Ask yourselves the following questions:

1. How much help will be required for ADL (activities of daily living) such as dressing, bathing, eating, toileting, and so on?

2. Will we be able to handle it alone?
3. If not, who will help?
4. Who will relieve us so we can have some time to ourselves?
5. Is our physical health up to looking after someone who has suffered a stroke?
6. Can he be left alone? If not, who will stay with him while everyone is at work or school?
7. Do we physically have space to house another person? If not, what changes would have to be made?
8. Is our home safe for someone with his particular limitations? If not, can we make it safe?
9. Who will take him to medical appointments?
10. Will he feel isolated living with us away from friends and former activities?
11. Do we have other home responsibilities, such as infants, toddlers, or a chronically ill child, that might interfere with his care?
12. How good was our relationship with this person *before* his stroke?
13. Do we all have patience, understanding, and a good sense of humor?
14. Can we afford to care for him at home?
15. Are we emotionally able to handle the increased stress of having him living with us?
16. Is our home really the best place for him?
17. Do we all really want him to move in with us?
18. Are we willing to make the sacrifices it will require?
19. Why do we want him to come live with us?
20. What are our other options?

If, after discussing these and other questions, everyone in the family is united in wanting the stroke survivor to live with them, you will need to prepare quickly for his arrival.

It isn't all bad, you know. Many parents say they are pleased by the depth of compassion and sense of responsibility their children develop toward the grandparent or other family member who moves in with them. It can bring a multigenerational family closer together when everyone works toward a common goal. It also can provide some wonderful moments of rediscovering what is so special about someone you love. Just be realistic and remember that life is not a movie or television special. Even in the best of situations, there is bound to be stress, tension, and fatigue as you all learn to reorient your lives in one household around the special problems that come with someone who has had a stroke.

Analyzing Your Physical Surroundings

Your family member may experience some physical limitations since his stroke that require awareness and preplanning on your part. If he needs a wheelchair, for example, you probably will have to widen the doorways to permit the wheelchair to move through them. Although the average wheelchair is about twenty-eight inches wide, some are narrower and even fold up slightly to allow passage. If your relative is slight, you can get a child's chair, which is smaller and lighter, a fact you'll appreciate when you try to lift the wheelchair into the backseat of your car.

You also need to install a ramp if you have a step-down living room or family room. You may need to remove some furniture to make room for a hospital bed if he requires one. If you use a regular bed, be sure it doesn't roll when the stroke survivor gets out of it, as he may be unsteady on his feet. It also needs to remain stable if the person is transferring from the wheelchair to the bed or vice versa.

If the stroke survivor has speech problems, the telephone—once a friend—becomes an enemy to be overcome. You may need to get an answering machine to take all calls if he is alone in the house. If speech isn't a problem but one hand is paralyzed, you might want to consider getting a push-button phone rather than one that requires dialing.

Depending on your family member's condition, you may

need to rearrange living quarters in the house, moving someone out of a downstairs bedroom to make room for the stroke survivor or even putting a bed in the family room or dining room. These and other changes are bound to be traumatic for the entire family. Even if you have to use screens or curtains, try to maintain a semblance of privacy for everyone involved.

Young children may be confused and even frightened by a familiar family member who now just stares into space and can't eat properly or move around without help. Teenagers, who need privacy at this period in their life, may resent having to share a room with a sibling so Grandpa or cousin Sue can have theirs. If at all possible, try not to restructure living arrangements so that your teenager is forced to share a room with the stroke survivor.

Falling and the fear of falling is a common problem for those suffering from residual effects of a stroke. Loss of balance, visual deficits, weakness, fatigue, side effects of medication, and gait problems all lend themselves to the real possibility of a fall. You can, however take precautionary measures to make your home safer for the stroke survivor. Such a list should include:

- removing scatter rugs that might cause a fall
- marking steps with colored tape
- installing grab bars in the tub and shower and by the toilet
- relocating or taping down extension cords that might cause a fall
- picking up toys, shoes, and other litter that could be tripped over
- keeping pets and toddlers out of the stroke patient's path
- putting night lights in the hall, bedroom, and bathroom
- replacing low-wattage light bulbs with higher ones near stairs

- clearing space around sturdy chairs so the person can move the wheelchair up to the chair and transfer into it safely

If the stroke survivor uses a wheelchair, go around the house in the wheelchair yourself before he moves in. Things look different from that angle, and you'll have a better idea of what needs to be changed. Kitchen glasses placed in a cupboard over the sink and the top shelf of the refrigerator may be too high to reach. Dresser drawers much over three and a half feet high may now be beyond reach. It's easy to rearrange cupboards, refrigerator shelves, and dresser drawers so that the most important items are easily accessible. The stroke survivor needs to feel as independent as possible and be encouraged to do things for himself. A little pre-planning on your part can help. This also prevents your doing unnecessary work.

Don't Do Too Much

Most of us err by being overhelpful, doing too much for the stroke survivor, who is trying to feel capable and independent. If he has come from the rehabilitation center, he has spent much time and energy learning how to do as much for himself as possible. He needs to do this for his own self-image.

If he has come directly to your home from the hospital, he needs to feel that he is not an invalid, that he is getting better and is able to care for himself, even if it's just the simple act of unfolding a napkin or wheeling his chair. If you try to do it all for him, he may become frustrated with his laborious efforts and give up trying.

Acknowledge that you may be overdoing your efforts to make things easier and ask your relative to let you know if he's feeling frustrated by your quick-on-the-draw helping hand. Admit that it takes time to know when to offer aid and when to stand back.

Making the Stroke Survivor Feel at Home

Encourage open discussion with the stroke patient before the homecoming in order to prepare both of you for the adjustments you will be making. Admit your concerns.

"Things will be different once you move in, but I know we can work together on any problems. I'm just glad you're coming home," is a good way to begin. Chances are the stroke survivor also has fears. The thought of moving into your home may be as overwhelming to him as how you're going to manage to juggle everything is to you.

If the stroke survivor is your parent, chances are he or she has always dreaded the thought of being a burden to you. Now the unthinkable has happened. It's painful. It makes a parent feel old and useless. Regardless of what your relationship has been—warm and loving or polite and careful truce—it is a big adjustment.

Even if the stroke survivor is confused and seems unaware of the coming move, it's still a good idea to talk about it. "We've moved a bed downstairs for you now, so you'll be closer to our room." Although he might not acknowledge what you've said, he may understand it nevertheless and have a better sense of place.

Try to make the person's room appear as familiar as possible. The patient may seem a little dazed and fatigued when he first comes home from the hospital or rehabilitation center, and familiarity can be comforting. Decorate the bedroom with his favorite painting, piece of sculpture, or quilt to make it seem less like a guest room and more like home. Family pictures offer a sense of place and trigger pleasant recollections. They're always good topics of conversation, especially when you've said all you can about the weather.

Moving into anyone else's house can be traumatic under the best of circumstances. Add to that the extreme fatigue that comes with having a stroke, the fear of dying, the loss of speech, physical dexterity, and, in some cases, bodily functions, as well as possible visual difficulties, depression, and actual damage to mental processes, and you'll have an idea why the stroke survivor seems less than enthusiastic about all the trouble you have gone through to make him comfortable in your home.

Remember also that your home may seem strange, especially after the routine of the hospital. There will be unfamiliar sounds from the street, noises from children or pets, ticking clocks, and those unique creaks and squeaks peculiar to your dwelling that you don't even hear anymore. In addition, your normal schedule is probably a hectic one. Many stroke patients take longer to process information than they did before. They really may be baffled by what seems like total confusion to them and are just your daily tasks to you.

If breakfast time is chaotic, offer your family member juice in his room and wait breakfast, if possible, until the horde has departed. If you have to get him fed before you run off to work yourself, try serving his breakfast on a quiet porch, TV room, or even in the bedroom.

Admit that you feel the stress, too. If possible, urge your family member to express what he is feeling. You're both in this together. There's no use pretending nothing's different. You both know it is. And you'll both feel better expressing it.

"Dad, I know this seems like a madhouse. But it's your home too now, and everyone in it loves you," is how one woman with three small children expressed it to her father. He just nodded and reached out for her hand. It didn't change the noise level of three small active youngsters and two rather large dogs, but it did ease the frustration level for this young woman and her father.

If you have difficulty expressing your feelings, you might want to talk to your religious leader, a psychologist, or a social worker. Don't deny the stress. It's there.

Bringing the stroke survivor into your home is an emotional event for everyone. Even if it's someone who has stayed with you before, there will be constant reminders that life is different this time, even in the same surroundings.

Encouraging Open and Honest Communication

"My son understood why his aunt was living with us," said a mother of three. "But he became very angry at the toll it was taking on me. I got so I hated to admit I was tired or depressed with the added burden of caring for my sister because it upset my son so and made him mad. Keeping all my emotions inside were even worse. It just made me more tense than I already was."

Although, as stated before, it's important to have a family meeting before the stroke survivor moves in with you, it's even more important to keep things on a routine basis once he's moved in. Let everyone air his or her gripes. Talk about the changes that have been made and how everyone feels about them. Discuss what new changes must be made. Encourage suggestions for ways to reorganize the house to make it easier for everyone—the stroke survivor as well as the other family members.

Urge the young people to express their fears and anger as well as to ask questions. Their former life-style is affected by the family member's stroke too. There may not be room for them to entertain their friends now, or you may be constantly telling them to quiet down and lower the volume of their stereos. You may be so busy with all the extra responsibility of caring for the stroke survivor that you don't have time or energy left for them. Ask them. Usually, if asked, they'll tell you the truth. Too often we adults get so caught up in our own emotions and the realities of daily life that we unconsciously shut out the young people. Even small children sense tension in a family. By talking about it, even in the simplest way ("Mommy's upset because Grandpa's been sick. Now that he's staying with us, things are a little different") is helpful.

Scheduling Time Out

Often, the primary caregiver feels guilty for wanting help and tries to handle everything alone. Homemakers with "plenty of time" may feel (rightfully so) dumped on by the rest of the relatives.

Don't play Superman or Superwoman. Plan ahead and actually schedule "days off" so that the burden of care doesn't rest on one person's shoulders. Teenagers can be extremely helpful in offering respite to a weary amateur nurse, when given the proper instructions, responsibility, and encouragement. They also may enjoy playing teacher and helping with the speech and physical therapy.

It's important to continue the work begun at the hospital and rehabilitation center. Too often that important part of a patient's care gets omitted because of a time crunch. After all, you have to feed, help bathe, and dress your loved one. If something has to go, it's often the lessons. Yet what makes these so vital is their very repetition. Younger children might enjoy helping out with some of the speech therapy, and many stroke survivors admit they don't feel at all self-conscious doing those lessons with their kids or grandchildren.

If you have siblings or other relatives in town, divide the responsibilities among them. Ask them to spell you on specific days or hours so you can maintain some life of your own as well. Friends of the stroke survivor would probably be pleased if you asked them to spend a few hours keeping him so you could get away.

Let your friends pitch in, too. They often feel frustrated and helpless by not knowing what they can do to help. You, on the other hand, may be equally frustrated by constantly being told, "If there's anything I can do, let me know. . . ."

So speak up. Be specific. "Yes, you can help. Would you stay with Uncle Joe Saturday afternoon at two? I want to see Sammy's soccer game." The time off from responsibilities will refresh you, make your friend feel good to be helping in a concrete way, and may even be good for Uncle Joe, who was, quite frankly, probably getting tired of seeing just your face, even though he couldn't speak well enough to tell you so. Chapter 12 includes many more suggestions on how to work with family and friends.

Sometimes, however, even with your best intentions,

things don't work out with your family member living with you. It becomes too much for you and your family to handle; he needs more care than you can give; you can't find adequate help in your community. You find yourself in a corner, staring at a wall. It seems as though the graffiti on it reads, "Nursing home."

7

When "Home" Must Be a Nursing Home

Our grandparents whispered the word "cancer," fearing that if they spoke it aloud, the disease might spread. We may not whisper "nursing home," but the words fill us with equal dread. To many of us, even the thought of someone we love living in a nursing home leaves us guilt-stricken, as though we didn't care enough or love enough to find another way.

Despite our preconceptions, a nursing home need not be the last stop, a depository for those waiting to die. Ideally they offer care and comfort while encouraging their residents to lead as active lives as possible. Most have social directors whose job it is to plan a varied schedule of activities—from wheelchair square dancing to bingo, outings to zoos and concerts, birthday parties, and exercise classes.

The fact is, however, that even the best nursing home is not what we really want for someone we love. We want them home; in truth we want them as they used to be—vibrant, healthy, interested in us and in our lives.

What to Expect

When my father suffered his debilitating stroke four years ago, the doctor took us—Daddy's three grown children—aside and urged us to begin looking at nursing homes. "You can't let your mother keep trying to care for him at home," he said. "It'll kill her. And knowing your dad, he won't let a nurse or aide or anyone else come near him as long as she's there."

He knew my father well. But Mother was his patient, too. He had treated her during both her coronary and her bout with cancer. He knew she was exhausted; her nursing days were done. Torn between conflicting loyalties to our parents, we agreed that a nursing home was the only solution.

The hospital social worker gave us a list of three local nursing homes that might have openings. As with the top colleges, the "best" nursing homes always have waiting lists. We were warned that none of the facilities on our list were easy to get into.

We talked with friends about their experiences in selecting a nursing home. "Don't expect to find one you really like," we were warned. "You take the best of what's available."

"Brace yourself for the smell," someone else said. "It hits you as soon as you open the door. It's an overwhelming urine smell, like the scent of our babies' diaper pail before the days of disposable diapers." She added, "My brother used to rub Vicks VapoRub under his nose so he wouldn't smell anything else when we went to visit our mother."

Another experienced nursing home visitor offered only reassurance. "My parents were in a wonderful nursing home," he said. "Everyone was kind, gentle, and considerate. We couldn't have been happier with our choice."

Somewhat encouraged by additional positive comments and strengthened by the fact that, for once, all three of us were in agreement, we set our appointments, dressed up so we'd look like responsible adult children of someone they'd want in their nursing home, and went for our interviews. Most of them went well. We asked polite, mildly probing questions. We answered the directors' questions about our father almost in unison, stressing his sense of humor, his interest in people, and his love of stamp collecting; we said nothing of his temper, demands to be waited on immediately, or sulkiness.

We took a tour of the facilities. A few of the residents were playing bingo. Some were sitting in wheelchairs, listening as a volunteer read the newspaper. Others were resting in their rooms. Everything was clean and pleasant. There was, to our great relief, no smell.

To our immense joy, we were accepted at our first choice. We felt like high school seniors, relieved and embarrassed at our delight in being wanted.

We bought a dresser and bookcase to make our father's room seem more personalized and collected favorite family pictures for his walls. We ordered name tags and an indelible marker to mark his clothes so the laundry could return them. Why did it seem like only yesterday that he had helped similarly in getting us ready for camp?

My father was transferred from the acute care hospital to the nursing home by ambulance. I volunteered to ride with him. I sat by his side, telling him that he was going to a lovely nursing home, that his clothes were already waiting for him there, that he'd know a few of the other residents. . . . I chattered on, painfully aware that I was talking to keep him from asking any questions and to keep me from thinking about the fact that I was transporting the father I loved to a nursing home where he would live out the rest of his life, and that I hated what I was doing.

Where were the bingo players? I wondered about that as I walked beside the stretcher the paramedics pushed, taking my father to his room in the nursing home. The dining room was empty now. The halls, however, were full, filled with patients sitting in their wheelchairs, waiting for lunch to be served. Some stared vacantly, some smiled and nodded as I walked by. One frail little woman with eyes shut tightly and hands upraised cried out in a shrill voice, "Did you come to take me home? Did you come to take me home?" The doll in her lap stared up at me as I hurried by. I couldn't take her home; I couldn't even take my own father home.

But he seemed comfortable and content, for the most part, in the nursing home. Although he couldn't (or wouldn't) ring the bell when he wanted them, the nurses and aides popped in often. He was always scrubbed, shaven, and dressed when I came by, which was anytime from eleven A.M. to six P.M., although visiting hours officially didn't begin until two P.M.

For a while he continued with the physical therapy he had been having in the hospital. Then the therapist told us that he was making no progress. He had done the unforgivable, as far as Medicare was concerned. He had "plateaued." He was making no progress, and despite the fact that he might, in time, Medicare would no longer pay for the therapist's services.

"We'll pay you privately," we offered. She smiled, then told us gently to save our money. It was her professional opinion that he'd get no better. His painful shuffling along behind a walker was the best he could do, would ever do. We stared back at her. This was the best, from my father, who had beaten every one of us kids in swimming matches in the pool?

This was the moment, I believe, that I finally realized the permanency of the damage caused by my father's stroke. From then on I realized the futility of pretending that things were as they had been or that eventually he'd return to the bantam rooster image I had of him.

Stroke patients in nursing homes often continue for a period to receive both the physical and speech therapy begun at the hospital. Some stroke survivors progress sufficiently to be able to cope with their limitations and return to their former homes with some assistance or move into the home of a family member.

Unfortunately, Medicare payments for valuable therapy is cut off when the patient plateaus and the therapist must report lack of progress, despite the fact that many patients improve, then plateau, pause, then improve some more. Just as every child has his own schedule for pulling up off his knees and taking his first teetering steps—I walked at nine months, my sister at sixteen months—Medicare in its bureaucratic wisdom assumes that every stroke patient progresses in exactly the same manner. The result: when the patient plateaus, the money goes. The family then must either pay for the therapist on their own or accept that future improvement is unlikely.

Nursing Home Costs

As of January 1, 1989, Medicare pays for a skilled nursing facility for 150 days. At first glance this seems encouraging financially. Then you consider the facts. Many stroke survivors don't require *skilled* nursing care, but rather general custodial care, which is not covered by Medicare. Stroke patients under sixty-five usually are not eligible for Medicare at all. In addition, stroke patients in nursing homes usually end up staying longer than Medicare's limit of 150 days. Furthermore, monies that are received often fall far short of the fees actually being charged by a particular nursing home facility.

Medicare requirements are ever-changing, and any nursing home cost estimates quoted as this book is written may be obsolete by publication. However, you should probably expect to pay about $100 a day and upward—way upward—for nursing home care. To receive the accurate updated information you need about Medicare and nursing home costs in order to make informed decisions, contact your local Social Security office and the office manager of any nursing home you are considering. For a comprehensive guide to your Medicare hospital and medical insurance benefits, call the 800 number listed in your phone book for Social Security and ask for your free copy of *The Medicare Handbook.*

Financial concerns are very real when someone you love is in a nursing home. For that reason, many people fall prey to insurance salesmen selling high-priced policies with uncertain benefits. Experts caution against the purchase of insurance plans that promise automatic full payment for everything, regardless of the type of care your loved one may require.

When you get rates from a particular nursing home, be sure to ask what that includes and *get it in writing*. Basic monthly rates may, indeed, be very basic. Usually items such as medications, bandages, adult diapers, razors, tissue, laundry, and so forth are billed as "extras." These can add up at an alarming rate.

Visits from the physician, dentist, barber, and podiatrist usually are billed separately as well. Since many stroke survivors also have other illnesses, such as diabetes, high blood pressure, and visual or coronary problems, medical and drug bills can mount. Once Medicare coverage runs out, you must pay privately as long as possible. Only when the patient's finances are exhausted can you then apply for Medicaid benefits so Medicaid can assume the burden.

How odd that financial aid of this type comes only when the patient is impoverished, rather than earlier in an illness when extra funding might help the stroke survivor remain in his own home or support the efforts of the family who struggle to share their home with their loved one.

How to Select a Nursing Home

Depending upon where you live, you may have little choice or a wide variety of nursing homes from which to choose. Unfortunately everyone wants to get their family member in the better nursing homes, so those facilities usually have waiting lists.

Where to Begin

1. Ask the stroke survivor's physician.
2. Contact the hospital social worker.
3. Ask your religious leader.
4. Check with friends who have family members in nursing homes.
5. Contact local senior centers.
6. Contact the Visiting Nurses Association.
7. Call your local medical association.

What Are the Different Types of Nursing Homes?

1. Nonprofit, which may be run by churches or synagogues or other organizations.
2. Profit-making, run directly by local or national companies or as a franchised operation.

One is not necessarily better than another. Your loved one may feel more comfortable in a facility where most of the residents are of the same faith so he or she can attend familiar religious services or have kosher food. A bilingual facility would appeal to someone whose native tongue—not English—was spoken by much of the staff as well as other residents.

A smaller nursing home may give more of a sense of family. On the other hand, a larger facility may be able to offer more activities and services. Some nursing homes are part of total adult housing complexes, where people rent or purchase apartments elsewhere on the grounds, knowing that the nursing facility is available for them if they become ill or disabled.

If you're fortunate enough to have a wide selection of nursing homes from which to choose, consider which facility would be the best "match," if other more important factors such as care, safety, cost, and location are equal.

What Factors Should Be Considered?

1. **Quality of care**

   You need to spend time talking with families of other residents of a particular nursing home and with the residents themselves, and keep your eyes open when you visit in order to determine this elusive factor called "quality of care."

   It incorporates many things: whether or not the residents are dressed or still in pajamas and bathrobes at midday; if the men have been shaved and the women helped with their hair and grooming; how the nurses and aides relate to the residents; whether there's gentle bantering or a coldness; whether bowel and bladder training is carried on or the residents are all in adult diapers; if there are activities or the residents remain passive, staring at television or into space; and how you feel about what you see.

2. Cost

It's unfortunate that cost must be a deciding factor in selecting a nursing home for someone you love, but it is a reality of life. Costs vary according to geographic location and the type of physical plant and facilities, but "more expensive" doesn't always mean "better." Some nursing home administrators seem more concerned about the appearance of their facility than the care its residents receive. Nevertheless, few families can afford to spend $30,000, $40,000, or even more a year for nursing home care. If your first choice costs $40,000 and your second "only" $20,000, you may have to go with your second choice. Unfortunately nursing homes don't offer scholarships like colleges.

3. Cleanliness

A tidy environment is not only important for your family member's morale, but it is also a health consideration. Overflowing trash cans in the rooms, dirty and overflowing laundry hampers in the hallways, and grimy doors and walls should make you wonder about the quality of care your relative would receive in that particular facility.

4. The facility's proximity to you

If the nursing home's location is convenient for you, you'll drop in more often rather than spending fewer but lengthier visits. Not only is that good for your loved one's morale (even if he or she doesn't appear to know you're there), but you can also judge the facility more realistically, seeing it as it is, not as it presents itself during special visiting days.

If you live out of town, ask a friend to make periodic spontaneous checks for you. Give them the checklist in Illustration F to complete and mail back to you.

Long-Distance Nursing Home Observation Report

Name of nursing home: _____ Date visited: __/__/__

Resident visited: _____ Time of Day: _____

RESIDENT'S CONDITION
(please check off as appropriate)

__In bed	__Taking part in activities (if so, what?) _____	Alert: __yes __no
__In wheelchair		Emotional State: (describe)
__Sleeping	__Dressed	
__Awake	__Still in nightclothes	Well groomed? (i.e. shaved, hair done, etc.) __yes __no

STAFF

Caring? __yes __no   Gentle with resident? __yes __no

Cheerful? __yes__no   Took time to talk with resident? __yes__no

RESIDENT'S ROOM

Clean? __yes __no   Plants or flowers cared for? __yes __no

Bed made if resident not in it?   Odor Free? __yes __no

__yes __no   Clothes clean & properly stored? __yes __no

FOOD

Adequate? __yes __no   Was resident helped with feeding, if necessary?

Appetizing? __yes __no   __yes __no __help not needed

Date of physician's last visit: __/__/__   Findings: _____

Resident's physical appearance, attitude, and morale: _____   Observer's name: _____

Is this different from your last visit? _____   Address and phone number: _____

Observer's suggestions: _____

If you don't know anyone there, you should be able to find a responsible person through the community's social services, a local college, or nearby retirement center who would serve as your representative.

Some families feel that proximity to a particular nursing home isn't as important as the facility itself. "I drove four hours each way every other weekend to see my father," a fifty-year-old man told me. "I did it for five years and I've never been sorry. It was the only choice I had. There was no Jewish nursing home here, and that was important to him—to me, too. It was an excellent nursing home. Over those five years, the staff remained pretty much the same—even the lower end of the pay scale. I guess they felt at home there, too. I know my father did. My experience with a nursing home was a positive one."

5. Staff morale

Although state and federal regulations spell out the staffing requirements of a nursing home, many facilities nevertheless often find themselves shorthanded. Aides, who usually have little training for their low-paid jobs, rush from patient to patient, trying to care for those who need the most help first.

Take time to be friendly to and chat with these men and women, as they are the ones who do the majority of nonmedical caring for the patients, leaving actual medical care for the nursing staff. Be sympathetic to their problems and ask frankly if the facility is shorthanded and, if so, if it's a recent problem or was always the case. You can learn a great deal about the nursing home through the attitude and morale of these aides.

6. Licensing

Be sure the facility you're considering is licensed and approved by the state. That means they pass basic *minimum* state requirements regarding staffing, sanitation, safety, programs, and the physical plant itself. The administrator must be licensed by the state as well. If either the facility or the administrator is not licensed, keep looking.

If the nursing home receives Medicare and Medicaid funding, they also must be certified by federal standards. Ask to see this license if it isn't displayed. Remember, however, that approval is granted through periodic on-site inspections and that the quality of inspections may vary from person to person, depending upon who is doing the inspection and how able and interested they are.

7. Recommendations

Although few people are delighted with the nursing home they have selected—"It's the best in town, but it's far from perfect," more than one family member said with a sigh—you can learn a great deal talking to others whose family members are residents in a particular nursing home. Ask them to tell you what they like and dislike about the facility.

By talking to others, you'll learn about special celebrations and activities, particular kindnesses or attention from the nursing staff, or what to ask for to make your loved one more comfortable.

Most nursing homes, for example, have refrigerators on each floor where you can leave special snacks to satisfy your family member's cravings between meals. Once you know this, it's easy to stock it with your relative's favorite brand of ice cream or other treat.

By talking to others who have gone through the same emotionally draining and guilt-filled exercise you are now experiencing, you'll also learn which nursing homes to avoid, and why. Do remember, however, that one person may have had a bad experience with a nursing home because of an unfeeling nurse or aide (who may no longer be employed at that facility) or because their loved one was difficult to handle.

Some stroke survivors have spontaneous temper outbursts or are otherwise rebellious and may have needed to be restrained at times to keep them from falling out of their wheelchairs or climbing out of bed. They also may understandably resent the loss of control over their lives and just be making things difficult for everyone around them.

8. Facilities

There is, or should be, more to a nursing home facility than just the resident's bedroom and a dining hall. On the other hand, an impressive physical plant doesn't necessarily guarantee quality of care. Below is a partial checklist, although few nursing homes have all of these facilities and some may combine them:

- activity room (for meetings, religious services, dances, wheelchair square dancing, bingo, and so on)
- arts & crafts room (with tables for painting or pasting, looms, easels, and the like)
- physical therapy room or gym
- quiet room (where families can hold private parties with patient or nursing staff can meet with family members)
- garden (for residents to plant flowers or vegetables as well as stroll in safety or just sit in the sun and enjoy the beauty of nature)
- television room (large enough for wheelchairs as well as chairs)
- examination rooms (so patients in double rooms may be assured privacy with their physician)

9. Your "gut reaction"

Just as most people react instinctively to others they meet, you will have some type of reaction to the various nursing homes you visit. The administrators of one may make you almost feel apologetic for applying, while others give you a warm feeling of caring and concern for your family member. You may surprise yourself by feeling more comfortable and pleased by one specific facility even though it offers less glitter than another. It may be that the atmosphere is warmer or just that it seems a better fit for your family member.

Usually it's best to go with your instincts. It may not

be the "in" nursing home, but it may be the best for your stroke survivor's specific needs.

For a more extensive checklist of things to look for in a nursing home, write:

American Health Care Association
1201 L. Street, NW
Washington, D.C. 20005-4014
(202) 842-4444

Ask for their free booklet, *Thinking About a Nursing Home? A Consumer's Guide to Long-Term Care.*

Preparing the Stroke Patient for the Move

Don't expect anyone to be overjoyed by the news that he or she is being moved into a nursing home. Those who understand what you're saying may be extremely depressed to realize that one of their greatest fears is being realized.

"My mother was alert," a sixty-two-year-old woman said, tearing up at the memory. "She knew she was incontinent, was unable to dress herself, had difficulty swallowing, and could barely speak. She also knew I had my hands full with my husband, who had suffered a stroke almost at the same time as my mother. I think she knew I had no choice, but she kept saying, 'Why? Why?' It was so hard. I felt torn and so alone."

Many nursing homes make the transition easier by allowing residents to bring personal items from home. If this is permitted, bring a favorite dresser, quilt, or rocking chair to the room before the patient moves in.

One Picture Is Worth a Thousand Words

Bring pictures of the family, pets, a special vacation spot, or anything else that looks familiar. It helps the nurses and aides to initiate and stimulate conversation in the beginning. It also helps the resident to hang on to reality.

Mark Everything

Put the patient's name on everything, either with a permanent marker or camp-type name tags, as things have a way of disappearing in most nursing homes. Often they are taken, not by the help, but by the other patients.

"I was so embarrassed," a friend told me when I met her at my father's nursing home. "I had heard from the nurses that the other patients were missing things from their rooms. Mother hadn't lost anything that I knew of, so I just said it was a shame and forgot about it.

"Then I discovered a red sweater in her drawer that wasn't hers. I began looking through the rest of her dresser and discovered a number of items that didn't belong to her. I guess she just wandered into the other patients' rooms when they weren't there and helped herself. After that, I made it a habit every so often to check through her things.

"Before the stroke, she never would have done anything like that. She's just different now. In so many ways, it's not really my mother."

List Food Likes and Dislikes

Most nursing home staffs are aware of proper nutrition and want their residents to enjoy their meals. Although they can't do special cooking for every patient, they do accommodate special needs and preferences. If your family member is a picky eater, give the dietitian a list of her likes and dislikes, along with any known food allergies. Although most nursing home meals are nutritious, they usually aren't what we think of as home cooking or gourmet restaurant cooking. The food is often bland. In addition, the stroke patient may find it confusing to eat in a dining hall with so many other people. The noise from other residents talking or calling out may be so distracting that she forgets what the fork is for or how to use it. She may sit staring at her plate. Encourage her, however, to keep taking her meals in the dining hall rather than eating alone in her room.

Having said that, I must admit that it's easy to understand how someone can lose her appetite in the dining room of most nursing homes. I feel a profound sadness in seeing so many once vital and active people hunched over their plates like children in a nursery. Some have to be fed; others just shove food around on their plates as though they could make it disappear by moving it often enough. There is some conversation among residents, but much of it is one-way with no answer expected from a table mate.

Nurses and aides hurry from table to table, helping all who need it, wiping a mouth, cutting up food into small bits so no one chokes, and offering an encouraging word to those who go forth on their own. I silently applaud these unsung heroes, these amazing men and women who gently care for those we love in nursing homes, and chide myself for scheduling my visits after mealtimes.

If your family member has difficulty swallowing or facial numbness, which makes it difficult to feel food left in the cheek, be sure to remind the nursing staff so that someone can help them at mealtimes.

Add Reality Reminders

If you've ever been in the hospital, you know it's easy to get confused about what time of day it is and even forget the day and date. To help the stroke survivor cope with memory loss, add reality reminders such as a wall battery-operated clock with large Arabic numbers, a large calendar where you can circle special dates, and a subscription to the local newspaper. Even if your family member has difficulty reading, someone can read specific stories to him and he also can look at the pictures.

It also may help to get individual pictures of all the family and label them with a label maker or black marker pen. Hang them on a bulletin board near the entrance of the door. You also can have regular-size photographs blown up to poster size. Photographs can help the patient to remember everyone's name and also introduces the family to the nursing staff so that when relatives come to visit, they are already familiar faces.

Expect Some Depression

Regardless of how much you've talked up the strengths of the particular nursing home, your family member may feel a letdown once she's settled in. Stroke patients who have regained some speech often become mute, staring at you in what you're sure is an accusing way. Those in a shared room may mourn their privacy or wonder why no one has chased the intruder from their room. They fuss about the strangers who parade up and down in what they consider to be their halls. They may fight the routine, refusing to be dressed for breakfast or take part in group activities.

If you've ever been in the military, at camp, boarding school, or in any other type of institution, you may remember how frustrating it was to have to "rise and shine" when ordered, eat when meals were posted, and otherwise conform to rules and regulations. The stroke survivor feels this particular frustration along with the pain of being uprooted from familiar surroundings, unable to do many formerly simple tasks such as dressing, bathing, reading, or even speaking. In addition, there are so many strangers around. No wonder they're confused, frightened, and probably angry as well.

Speak to the head nurse if, after a week or so, you still feel the patient is depressed or pouting. You may discover, as we did, that often it's only for your benefit. Like a child who stops crying the minute the agonized parents leave the house, the newcomer to a nursing home may find the activities fun and even stimulating.

"Your dad's great," we were told. "He sings all the songs and doesn't want to leave even when the music time is over." And when *we* had quizzed him about the music program, all we got was a shrug.

It's been four years now that my father's home has been in the nursing home. On good days he jokes and flirts shamelessly with the nurses, tells me he's glad I came to visit, and struggles (and fails) to remember who I'm talking about when I tell him what my five kids are doing. He thanks me politely for rubbing his neck, trimming his mustache, and bringing him a McDonald's hot butterscotch sundae.

On bad days he says politely, "Shouldn't you introduce yourself?" He yells or doesn't talk to me at all. He looks at me without recognition, throws his medicine against the wall, and turns the ice-cream cup upside-down. The McDonald's soft ice cream with hot butterscotch sauce slowly drips down onto the black-and-white plaid blanket.

It's been four years now since my father entered a nursing home. He seems to have adjusted to life there. I thought I had adjusted to his being there as well. I was wrong.

A few months ago my husband and I went to see the touching play, *Driving Miss Daisy*. It's a moving story about an elderly southern woman and a black man who becomes her driver. It tells of how their friendship grows as they both age. In the last scene, Miss Daisy is in a nursing home. Her driver comes to visit her and brings her a piece of pumpkin pie. She's unable to eat it properly, so he gingerly feeds it to her as one might feed a child. As I watched, tears flooded my eyes and streamed down my cheeks. Deep sobs erupted. I fled.

=8=

Dealing with Communication Difficulties

Have you ever dreamed that you were hurt or in trouble and you tried to call for help, but nothing came out? Have you ever had laryngitis and been told to keep quiet for a week or more? Have you ever had a word or name just on the tip of your tongue but been unable to remember it? If so, you know just a fraction of the frustration a stroke patient feels on realizing that she can't speak, that she's lost the power to communicate.

"The worst part," my mother confided after she began to regain her speech, "was that I knew what I wanted to say. The words were there—in my head—but they wouldn't come out."

It's equally frustrating to the family. You feel that you've lost the closeness you once had with the person you love. If the patient doesn't understand what you're saying, you can't share your fears and dreams. You can't reassure or convey your thoughts. You feel as though you're talking through a one-way glass partition.

The stroke survivor may not speak at all, or he may talk in gibberish, making no sense. A person with a right-brain stroke may talk nonstop, interrupt, and otherwise behave like a hyperactive child. You may be exhausted by his excessive verbal flow. You may have a reasonable conversation with him at ten A.M., only to discover that by noon he's forgotten you had it. He may speak, but the words are so slurred that you can't figure out what he's saying. It's sad, frustrating, and depressing.

"I'm lonesome," admitted the older wife of a stroke survivor. "It's just the two of us in this big house now that the kids are grown. We looked forward to these years, to finally being alone with each other. I love him, but I was never the big talker in the family. He was. Now we have such long stretches of silence. I feel it screaming at me. I can't stand the thought that this is the way it's going to be for the rest of our lives together."

Communication problems are one of the most devastating effects of stroke because it drives a wedge between the patient and his family. The family feels unsure of how to know or satisfy the stroke survivor's needs, and the stroke survivor feels frustrated and lost. As Nancy L. Mace and Peter V. Rabins said in their book, *The Thirty-Six Hour Day*, "We sense that language is the most human of mental skills."[1] Without it, the stroke survivor is dependent, lonely, and suffers a severe loss of self-confidence.

In *The Man with a Shattered World*, A. R. Luria wrote, "Apart from being a means of communication, language is fundamental to perception and memory, thinking and behavior. It organizes our life."[2]

What Causes Communication Problems?

The brain is divided into equal halves. The left hemisphere controls functions on the right side of the body, and vice versa. Somewhat specific and predictable communication difficulties arise depending upon which side of the brain received the damage. For most right-handed people, the left side of the brain is the language center. Communication problems come in a variety of patterns that may fluctuate

1. Nancy L. Mace and Peter V. Rabins, M.D., *The 36-Hour Day* (Baltimore: The Johns Hopkins University Press, 1981), 29.
2. A. R. Luria, *The Man with a Shattered World* (New York: Basic Books, Inc. Publishers, 1972), 33.

even from hour to hour. But it isn't just speech that's affected, but the entire spectrum of what we call "communication."

Communication is far more than just what we say. It has a two-way component: 1) expressive, or what we do and say to communicate; and 2) receptive, or what we understand when others communicate to us.

Expressive communication includes:

- speech
- gestures
- facial expressions
- writing
- counting
- handling of mathematics

Receptive communication includes:

- getting meaning from the gestures of others
- understanding what others say to us
- getting meaning from the printed page (as with reading)
- accepting the concept of time from a clock or watch

Most stroke survivors have difficulties in one or more areas of both expressive and receptive communication. Deficits can range from extremely mild to most severe. The problems also can fluctuate so that the patient may communicate his thoughts at one time and be incapable of expressing anything the next. It's hard to accept how he could have spoken rather clearly one day when his speech is garbled or nonexistent the next. You begin to wonder if he's being contrary or lazy. Both the stroke patient and those who care about him live in a state of uncertainty surrounded by anxiety.

When I first realized that Mother's stroke had left her unable to speak, I made the layperson's common mistake. I assumed that she would at least be able to write what she wanted to say, much as the person with a vocal cord disability does. I even thought—creatively, I felt—about getting her a typewriter, Scrabble board, and other spelling devices. What I hadn't understood is that the stroke doesn't just affect the voice, as laryngitis does. It damages the part of the brain that creates speech, helps us remember and recall words, puts meaning to words, letters, and gestures, and moves the muscles of the vocal cords, lips, and tongue that form our words.

What Are the Communication Problems?

Damage to the speech center of the brain acts like radio interference, causing static so that the stroke patient may be unable to coordinate the muscles of the diaphragm, throat, tongue, and lips to form words—or it may interfere with word recall, like a word-processing machine with a defect, so that "cup" may be called up when the person means to say "water," or a nonsense word rather than one that has meaning.

Strokes create a number of baffling phenomena in the speech area. With those who are multilingual, for instance, the memory and ability to speak all but the native language may be wiped out. A stroke survivor may lose the ability to speak but sometimes be able to sing, because those words are learned by rote, just as we often automatically say, "God bless you," when someone sneezes. A musician may lose the ability to read notes but be able to read words.

Specific problems are broken down into categories, although the range of severity fluctuates greatly from individual to individual.

Aphasia

Aphasia, as mentioned previously, is a general term for speechless or impaired communication due to brain dysfunction in the center that handles speech. Although it signifies difficulty with speech, aphasia has nothing to do with a lessening of intelligence. Thousands of extremely bright people are imprisoned by stroke into silent bodies, leaving them unable to communicate what is in their still functioning minds.

A stroke survivor with aphasia may

not speak at all

If this lasts only a few days, it is called transient aphasia. On the other end of the continuum, if the stroke survivor is unable to speak and seems to understand nothing that is said to him, the condition is termed global aphasia. This is the most severe type of aphasia because the person is truly isolated and most horribly alone.

say some words on impulse, but not on command

The patient may say "bye" when you leave, but when you hurry back into the room, overjoyed, he is unable to repeat it for you. With this type of aphasia, the stroke survivor may also repeat words over and over again, like a broken record. This condition is called perseveration. It may take the form of a sentence, such as "I don't know"; counting, which is a rote type of speech; or even cursing. This may embarrass your family tremendously if your sweet old mother begins swearing at the minister. But she can't help it or, as often is the case, may not be aware that she is doing it.

speak only single words, usually nouns

This is the type of beginning speech we hear from toddlers. They may say "dog" or "milk" and leave us to fill in the verbs, adjectives, and other parts of speech. Some aphasics have the same speech pattern. It is, however, extremely important to remember that these stroke survivors are *not* toddlers. They are adults, and despite the fact that their speech is on a two-year-old level, they have adult minds.

Never talk down to someone with aphasia, and certainly do not talk baby talk to them. (For that matter, you probably shouldn't speak it to the toddler, either.)

speak, but use the wrong words

With this type of speech deficit, the stroke survivor may say "door" but mean "window." He may use "thing" instead of the noun he means and wave a hand, leaving you to wonder what he is trying to say. The person may become angry when you don't understand, which makes you feel more guilty, angry, and frustrated. It is very confusing for the family because we want so very badly to talk to the person we love. The patient also may say "yes" when he means "no," without being aware of it, and may become angry when you react to what he said, not what he *meant* to say.

One man remembered that, after his father's stroke, his father always said "no" when he asked if the doctor had been in to see him. Feeling frustrated (as well as frightened and angry), the son stormed into the nurses' station to complain about the unfeeling physician who had ignored his father. The nurses finally were able to soothe him by showing him the doctor's notes. The doctor had, indeed, been in every day, but the father had mixed up the words "yes" and "no."

A person with aphasia also may nod, smile, and seem to understand what is being said to him when he really doesn't. In a way he may be trying to appease those around him and to keep them from knowing he doesn't understand what they are saying. He may be frightened that he's gone "crazy" and doesn't want anyone to suspect.

He also may only hear parts of a sentence or question and respond to those words he understands. For example, when you ask, "Do you want to get up?" he may only hear, "Do up?"

speak in an abbreviated form

With this type of problem, known as telegraphic speech, the patient speaks in a kind of shorthand, omitting prepositions, articles, and conjunctions, the so-called little words. He may say, "Joe bring belt." It's a bit easier to understand someone with this type of deficit, but improvement still is desirable, if possible.

hear the words, but not understand the meaning

Although stroke does not affect hearing as such, it can damage the area of the speech center that affixes meaning to the sound of the words we hear. Shouting at the patient only confuses him because, although you're louder, he still can't understand what you're trying to say. It's like yelling at a foreigner who doesn't understand English. No matter how loudly you scream, volume won't translate your words into something with meaning.

be unable to recognize letters or read

This deficit leaves the stroke patient looking vainly at letters on a page that are devoid of meaning for him. He might be able to recite part of the alphabet, as that is learned by rote and is automatic for most of us. But a person with this problem cannot attach symbolic meaning to any of the words he sees. This may be difficult to spot because your family member may stare intently at a newspaper for hours. You may think he's reading and, trying to be helpful, bring magazines and even books. But you may be fooled. He may not understand a single word.

be unable to write

There doesn't have to be a problem with the stroke patient's hand for him to be unable to write, although some people do have paralysis with their dominant hand and have to be trained to use the other hand. With this type of aphasia, the stroke survivor can't remember how to form the actual letters. The connection from the brain to the muscles of the hand has been damaged. He may be able to think of a word but have no idea how to write it. The act of writing also includes forming sentences and using the proper syntax. That ability may be lost as well.

As writing ability is the last communication skill we learn as children, it usually is the last to return after a stroke. Most aphasics have difficulty in at least one aspect of the writing process, and many have some degree of permanent deficit.

be unable to use gestures properly

This type of deficit can drive a family crazy because as the patient waves his hand, we run over to see where he's pointing, what he wants, and play all kinds of guessing games. The gestures are wrong for the action desired, however, and it's difficult to discern the message when the clues are wrong. It can cause a great deal of confusion when someone nods "yes" regardless of the question. He isn't doing it on purpose, however. It's the fault of the stroke.

be unable to understand the gestures of others

Closely linked to the above problem, this is a receptive problem. The stroke survivor can see you shake your head but doesn't remember what that gesture means.

In addition to the above aspects of aphasia, a stroke survivor may have combinations of these, such as being able to write but not being able to read what she has written, or being able to read words in the newspaper but having no understanding of what they mean.

Agnosia

People who have trouble with communication reception— understanding what is being said, recognizing letters, and so on—are said to have agnosia. They may stare at a brush or cup and not remember what it is for, as though the symbol or image storage center had been erased. They may have a problem understanding how to perform known activities such as dressing. They also may look at a familiar family member and have no recollection of having seen the face before. It's quite a shock when you first realize that your beloved parent or mate doesn't recognize you. My father once asked me politely, "Shouldn't you introduce yourself?" I did, adding that I was his youngest daughter.

It is not sudden senility, however, but a sensory deficit that may be reversible once the swelling has gone down in the brain and after proper therapy. Sometimes, however, it is a permanent condition.

Apraxia

Verbal apraxia is difficulty in expressing language, through speech, writing, gestures, and the like, because the body won't do what the mind wants it to. A person with verbal apraxia may know what he wants to say, but because of the damage created in a specific area of his brain, he is unable to voluntarily form his lips or move his tongue properly in order to make the sounds. It is somewhat like watching an aerobic instructor demonstrate a new dance step and finding that, when you try to repeat it, your brain knows what to do but your feet won't obey.

It's painful to watch someone you love struggling to form a word that is in his mind, especially when we, who haven't had a stroke, take it so for granted. You wait, unconsciously moving your own lips as though that could help.

There is another form of apraxia called motor apraxia, where the person can sit or stand spontaneously but cannot follow a request to do so.

Dysarthria

Many stroke survivors suffer from dysarthria, which can be due to a physical weakness in muscles used to shape sounds or control shaping of sounds. Dysarthria can cause difficulty in producing sounds, which creates the drunklike slurring of words we associate with someone who has had a stroke. It also causes the person's vocal intonation to change. Even more serious, along with dysarthria there can be problems in swallowing. Known as dysphagia, swallowing difficulties can affect the ability to chew and swallow food, which may lead to choking or aspirating food and liquid into the lungs. In severe cases the patient may have to be fed through a feeding tube to avoid aspiration pneumonia or choking.

Jargon

A patient with jargon aphasia sounds like a child with a made-up language. It may have the same rhythm and pausing as normal speech, but is unintelligible. The patient may say, "Ju durble keek tras," and look at you expectantly for your response. He may or may not realize that something is wrong with what he is saying.

How Can These Problems Be Treated?

Each of these communication problems has its own ways of being treated. The speech therapist works closely with the family, offering suggestions on how you can best help your family member to regain enough communication skills—through speech, gestures, writing, or whatever it takes—so that the stroke survivor won't feel so isolated.

Before my mother regained any speech, her speech therapist suggested that we try singing to her to see if she would join in spontaneously. Apparently the speech center of the brain is in a different area from the music center. Damage to one side doesn't necessarily affect the other. Determined to do whatever we could, my sister and I (both tone deaf and still chafing from being told in high school chorus to "just mouth the words, please") checked our meager musical repertoire and came up with "Three Blind Mice." We sat facing Mother and, feeling extremely self-conscious, began singing in our monotone best, the two of us hitting identical notes about twice. We got as far as "the child takes a . . ." and faltered. What *did* the child take? The dog? My mother shook her head. The cat, then? Again, she shook her head.

We felt quite embarrassed with our poor efforts. Mother reached for a piece of paper and a pen. In a scrawl, weak but legible, she wrote the letters *N-U-S-R*.

I felt like Anne Sullivan when the child Helen Keller said, "Waa-waa," in response to feeling water in her hand. Mother *was* communicating. She hadn't spoken, but she had written her equivalent of "nurse." She knew the words to that nursery rhyme better than her daughters did. At that moment I knew she would improve.

It Takes Time

But it comes slowly. The gift of speech is far more complex than any of us can ever imagine. So much is involved in the seemingly simple act of communication. The magic of the speech therapist comes in being able to understand the nature of each specific difficulty, to know how best to work with the individual patient, and then, patiently, encouraging and gently pushing without frustrating, to retrain layer upon layer of the speech process until, at long last, the stroke survivor is communicating in some fashion. It is not a speedy process, nor is it always a totally successful one.

In an article on stroke rehabilitation, researchers Joseph M. Wepman, Ph.D., and Lyle V. Jones, Ph.D., wrote, "The therapeutic challenge does not lie only in the ability of the language therapist, but with the whole team. The team should always include the family. The goals of therapy should never be expressed in terms of words that can be spoken, written, spelled, or put into sentences, but always in terms of the patient reacquiring the ability to communicate in any life situation. While our immediate concern is the language problem as found in the aphasic patient, recovery lies not only in the recovery of language, but also in the total integration of physical structure, medical condition, personality, and intellect."[3]

There are many types of possible communication disorders that are created by a stroke, with a wide variety of gradations in severity. Most stroke survivors don't have all of them; a few fortunate ones have none, but many patients have some type of difficulty in communication and point to this as the most trying aspect of surviving a stroke. It isolates them on an island of loneliness, cut off from the social contact they once enjoyed.

"I am aware that the phone doesn't ring much anymore," my mother, the pragmatist, told me. "People stop calling. It's hard to talk to me on the phone."

This sense of isolation permeated most of my conversations with stroke survivors, excepting only those with the

3. Joseph M. Wepman, Ph.D., and Lyle V. Jones, Ph.D., "Aphasia: Diagnostic Description and Therapy," in *Stroke Rehabilitation: Basic Concepts and Research Trends*, ed. William S. Fields, M.D. and William A. Spencer, M.D. (St. Louis: Warren H. Green, Inc., 1967).

most minor difficulty with their speech. As with the stutterer, well-intended friends try to help the stroke survivor by completing sentences, interrupting—although they would consider it rude doing the same thing to someone who had no speech difficulty—or, worse, just staying away.

"I don't know what to say," they rationalized. "I don't want to make her feel bad that she can't talk." It soon becomes a catch-22 situation: the stroke survivor has difficulty speaking because she has so little opportunity to practice what she learned in therapy, and she has little opportunity to practice because visitors stop coming now that she has trouble speaking. This is especially true for the stroke survivor who returns to her former home and is alone, except for family who comes to visit and the occasional helper.

What Does the Therapist Do?

The speech therapist usually arrives on the scene shortly after a person has suffered a stroke and the physician feels he is out of danger. The therapist should be a certified speech-language pathologist, which means he or she has a master's degree in speech pathology, has passed a national certification exam, and has completed a clinical fellowship year working under the supervision of an experienced speech therapist. Some states also require state licensing. Be sure the individual has worked with stroke survivors before, not just children with speech problems.

You don't need a doctor's prescription for a speech therapist unless insurance will pay for it. If your physician is reluctant to contact a speech therapist, you can check with your local hospital, rehabilitation center, Easter Seal organization, college or university with a speech pathology department, private practitioner, or by writing:

The American Speech-Language-Hearing Association
10801 Rockville Pike
Rockville, Maryland 20852
(301) 897-5700

Toll-free consumer number: 1-800-638-8255

For many stroke survivors, continued contact with the speech therapist—either as an outpatient at a clinic or on a home-visit basis—is their major source of social intercourse. "Most of us stick around longer than the other therapists," said speech therapist Leah Davidson, M.S., CCC. "The person needs to develop new pathways in the brain in order to relearn speech. It takes time and repetition. Never underestimate the amount of effort this requires."

If you've ever tried to learn a foreign language or a new dance step or to write with your nondominant hand, you only experienced a fraction of the effort, motivation, and frustration the struggle to regain speech requires. Each specific problem carries with it numerous unique difficulties. When the damage caused by the stroke is more extensive, it doubles or even triples the effort that must be made to regain even a slight form of communication.

The therapist tailors the specific therapy to the individual needs of each stroke patient, using material that has meaning for that person, such as sailing terminology for the sailing buff or sewing items for the seamstress; repetition; and carefully adapted homework assignments to reinforce what was learned in therapy. This helps the patient to retrain his brain to find new pathways for communication; keeps him busy when much of his former social and work activity has been curtailed; and allows the family to take an active part in the therapy, which helps the family unit interact and support one another.

Most therapy sessions last from about thirty minutes to an hour and are usually scheduled two or three times a week. The therapist and the stroke survivor work together, although sometimes a family member is asked to join them in order to observe or learn a particular technique so she can work with the patient later.

There are also intensive residential programs such as the University of Michigan's Residential Aphasia Program, which offers a six-week intensive speech and language therapy program for people who are

1. at least eighteen years of age;
2. ambulatory and physically capable of independently caring for their personal needs;
3. medically stable;
4. emotionally stable.

If you think your family member might be interested, write:

> The University of Michigan
> Residential Aphasia Program
> 1111 East Catherine Street
> Ann Arbor, Michigan 48109-2054
> Phone: (313) 764-8440

According to Ms. Davidson, a speech therapist tests the stroke survivor in six major areas:

1. *Expressive language*: how the person communicates through verbal means as well as gestures.
2. *Receptive language*: what they understand from the communication of others.
3. *Oral musculature movements*: how the tongue, lips, soft palate, and vocal cords work.
4. *Writing*: intelligibility of the written word and the ability to create a complete sentence.
5. *Reading*: comprehension.
6. *Swallowing*: how the patient is able to chew and swallow food, liquids, and saliva.

Naturally these tests are only useful when compared with the abilities the person had before the stroke. Someone who is basically illiterate won't test as well in the reading or writing areas as someone who has strong capabilities in those areas. The therapist also must know which abilities are still intact as well as what medications the patient is taking and their possible side effects, as medicine can do strange things to a person's personality. Older people also metabolize drugs more slowly, so the chemicals can build up and strengthen their effect.

Families often ask the speech therapist, "Will he get better?" when what they really mean is, "Will he speak again?" It's a difficult question for a therapist because there are so many unknown factors *in addition* to the amount of damage and area of damage from the stroke.

Age

Certainly the person's age is one factor. Not only do we tend to learn more slowly as we age, but older people also may have other physical and mental conditions that make relearning more difficult.

Motivation

Motivation is tremendously important. Learning to overcome communication deficits after a stroke is extremely hard. It takes a great deal of determination and effort for any success. That's where we, the family, come in. Our support and patience can help the stroke survivor to feel the effort is worthwhile.

It's hard, though. Just as it's easier to tie a child's shoelace than to wait for him to laboriously make the bow, it takes an enormous amount of patience to wait for someone—even someone we love very much—to think of a word, form it mentally, carefully place tongue and lips in the right position, and then utter it. You sit or stand, waiting, thinking of all the errands you have yet to run and the work that's piling up. You ache, mourning the loss of the once verbal and quick-witted person they were before the stroke. Yet you wait and try to be encouraging, because without it your family member understandably may become discouraged and give up.

Health Prior to Stroke

Naturally, health problems before the stroke may play some part in the patient's recovery. If there's deafness, for example, it may be difficult to ascertain if the stroke survivor doesn't respond because he can't hear the speaker or because he can't understand what the speaker is saying. A preexisting problem with vision may prevent the patient from seeing subtle gestures and facial expressions that could help supplement what is being said to him.

Personality

Although a stroke usually causes some personality changes, certain prestroke personality traits do show up and affect the therapy process. If your family member was negative and pessimistic by nature before the stroke, it isn't reasonable to expect that, with all the extra stress and difficulties brought on by the stroke, he will suddenly become easygoing and optimistic about therapy. Depression, which is frequent with those who have suffered a stroke, may worsen in those who were often depressed prestroke and also can interfere with the effectiveness of therapy.

What Can You Do to Help?

For the most part, you can trust your instincts. But below are a number of tips that others have found useful in helping communication between themselves and their family member.

Never Say Anything in Front of an Aphasic Person That You Don't Want Him to Know or That Might Be Misunderstood

An aphasic may be mute, but he can hear. A patient who can *not* understand may, at any moment, make the connection and be able to understand. A stroke survivor also may still be able to read, although he may have lost the ability to speak. When my mother was still in the acute care facility, she received a great many floral arrangements. My sister and I began reading aloud the cards that came with flowers, thinking she would be interested to know who had sent what. She kept grabbing for the cards and looking at them. Finally we asked timidly, "Can you read those cards?"

She looked at us with that look mothers give daughters who have said something idiotic. She nodded grimly. At first we didn't believe her. Finally, when she began to respond with gestures, we realized that her reading ability had not been affected by her stroke. We acknowledged our mistake, which, I think, relieved her. She later said, "It's terrifying to suddenly wake up and discover that you can't communicate. You feel so lost and alone."

Treat the Patient as Normally as Possible
Include him in a conversation, even if he doesn't respond. He may understand some or even all that is being said and will become more motivated if he feels he is still considered an important part of the family.

Encourage Friends to Visit
You may have to call and ask the stroke survivor's friends to visit him. It's not that they don't want to. Most people do, but they don't know how to act or what to say. They worry about what to do when he can't talk to them or they don't understand what he's trying to say. They don't realize that just by showing up, they reassure the stroke patient that he still has friends, is still an important part of their life, even though it may not seem like it to him just now. Chapter 12 deals directly with how to get help from friends and family.

Make Your Conversation as Workable as Possible
Keep background distractions to a minimum. Too many people cross-talking, loud music, laughter, television, and other noise jams the communication lines in the stroke patient who has suffered damage to the speech center of the brain.

I learned this firsthand, in a most vivid way, when I took my mother to a frozen-custard shop in our neighborhood. It was almost empty, so I thought we could have a nice relaxing talk. Unfortunately the manager decided we needed more atmosphere with our frozen calories, so he turned on his old-fashioned jukebox. The instant the music began blaring, my mother stopped speaking midsentence. It was like a circuit breaker clicking off when the circuit has been overloaded. It was most dramatic, and a good example of the concentration needed for the aphasic person's struggle to communicate.

When we are under stress or overtired, the weakest link deteriorates. With a stroke patient communication can be affected, so that a person who has been able to speak in short sentences may, when overtired, be able to utter only one- or two-word phrases. It also can happen to those of us who have not had a stroke as well. I once had the opportunity to interview Peter Falk (television's Columbo) after his performance in the Broadway show *Prisoner of Second Avenue*. I was ushered backstage to his dressing room, where he greeted me and motioned for me to sit down. I did. Then I opened my mouth to ask him my first question, but no sound came out. My nervousness had truly rendered me speechless for a few seconds. Is it any wonder, then, that fatigue and stress can play havoc with the stroke patient, who already is burdened with communication difficulties?

Encourage Writing, If Possible, To Supplement Speech

Remember that the goal of speech therapy is for the stroke survivor to be able to communicate, not to speak perfectly. If your family member is able to write a little, encourage him to keep a notebook or index card and pencil handy, so he can write down the words he can't get out. Between his speech, writing, and maybe a few gestures, he may be able to communicate a little better, which certainly gives rewards and adds motivation to his efforts.

My mother's speech therapist told us to get her a "speech notebook" early in her therapy. Dutifully, my sister and I scoured the town, only to return in defeat. Nobody knew what we were talking about. When we reported our failure to the therapist, she laughed.

"I didn't communicate so well myself," she said. "I meant a plain notebook for her to write on to supplement her speech."

Years ago my pediatrician told me to buy my first baby a "net blanket," which might help clear up the rash on her face. I looked all over town, but nobody had ever heard of one. I came back to his office to report. He shook his head, took a prescription pad, and wrote "knit blanket." His thick southern drawl had muddled his message. Obviously you don't have to have a stroke to have difficulty with communication.

Speak Slowly and Distinctly

Slow your speech down so the patient can follow what you're saying, but don't go so slowly that he becomes distracted or loses interest. Don't talk with food or gum in your mouth, as it distorts the sound.

The person with aphasia needs more time than usual to process what is being said. You may wonder if he has a hearing problem, but it's not that. Think of it as though you're hearing someone speak Spanish; not being fluent in the language, you must first mentally translate those words back into English before you're able to understand what's being said.

If people speak slowly and are patient, the stroke survivor will have unpressured time to process what's been said and find some, if not all, of the meaning.

Look at the Patient When You Speak

If she's having difficulty with reception, she may need to use your gestures or facial expression as additional clues to what you are saying.

Keep It Simple

Use simple sentences with one thought, rather than compound sentences. Don't say, "Do you want coffee, tomato

juice, or orange juice?'' Instead, ask, ''Do you want coffee?''

Use Gestures to Illustrate What You Are Saying

If you're asking about a cup of coffee, pantomime the act
of pouring coffee and drinking it.

Do *Not* Use Baby Talk

The stroke survivor may be as mute as a baby but is an
adult with adult feelings. Never talk down to him. His self-
image is shaky enough with the loss of speech, independence, physical abilities, and control over his life.

Don't use baby-type books with pictures of apples, cars,
and dogs, either. Although they might be useful aids, many
stroke patients will resent the inference. It's more supportive to paste magazine pictures on index cards, using photos
of adults, not children. The stroke patient's speech therapist
can help you find suitable material.

Use Familiar Pictures

If you use pictures and photographs to try to communicate, use those with personal significance. Don't show a
snow scene, for example, to a Sun Belt inhabitant when
you're talking about how cold it is. Take photographs of the
stroke survivor's bed, toilet, chair, table, family members,
and the like to illustrate what you are saying. He can then
point to a particular picture to express his needs, unless
there is a deficit with reception. In that case the person
might not identify his need with a particular picture because
the symbolic meaning of the picture is lost.

Encourage Talk with Siblings

Sometimes an older stroke patient will have spontaneous
speech with a sibling, even though he is mute with his
spouse and children. One of the reasons is that we share
common memories from childhood and these often trigger
automatic speech. The sibling may say, ''Remember that
old dog we had? What was his name? Trigger?'' and the

stroke survivor, to everyone's amazement, will pop in with, "It was . . . Tiger."

Lower Your Voice

There is a natural tendency to raise your voice when someone doesn't seem to understand. But nothing is wrong with the stroke survivor's hearing, so don't scream. Try to use a normal speaking tone or even lower it slightly.

Praise, But Don't Overdo It

Everyone needs encouragement, and it's helpful to give praise when the stroke survivor's struggle to achieve even a small victory has been successful. But don't overdo your praise. There's nothing wrong with the patient's intelligence, and he'll resent your praise when it doesn't ring true. It also will devalue it for another time.

Don't Do Too Much

Because we care so very deeply, the temptation is always to do more for the stroke survivor than we should. Although it's all right to get him started by cuing a sentence—"You want to eat some . . ."—don't anticipate every desire or he'll give up trying to finish the sentence.

It's important for him to try, even if he fails. Hopefully, as the brain heals and therapy progresses, he'll eventually have some successes. But if you help too quickly, by either trying to guess what he wants or completing the sentence, he won't bother to try.

When the person does attempt to say something, stop what you're doing and try to give him all your attention. Be aware of your body language, too, so you aren't tapping your fingers impatiently or nodding your head. If you can just wait, concentrate on relaxed breathing, and remember to smile, the stroke survivor may be able to get his sentence or, at least, express the thought.

If, despite his efforts, he can't express himself, acknowledge that he may have more success next time. Don't spend all afternoon waiting because you'll both get very frustrated.

Never Promise Perfection

Remember that the goal of speech therapy is to get the stroke survivor communicating. The chances are extremely high that he'll never have perfect speech again. Don't even wave that as a possibility. Instead, encourage communication so you can share and enjoy each other's company. Accept him with his limitations and encourage him to improve as much as possible within these limitations.

Admit When You Don't Understand

Don't try to bluff your way out. If your family member says something, but you can't even get the gist of it, say, "I'm sorry, Mother. I don't seem to understand what you want. Is it something about . . . ?"

She may either nod, which encourages you to begin narrowing the scope of the subject, or shake her head impatiently. If you meet an impasse, say, "I just can't seem to understand. I'm sorry. It makes me frustrated, too. Let's try again later."

Acknowledge the Speech You Do Hear

Whatever does come out when the stroke survivor speaks may not have anything to do with what he is attempting to say. For example, if he only says, "Car," respond with, "I hear you saying 'car,' but I don't know what you're thinking. Is it something about a car?" He nods or shakes his head. "Is it someplace you want to go in the car?" Even if you don't guess right, at least you give feedback to the person that you have understood what he is trying to say. It may be that he didn't mean "car" at all, but rather "garage" or "policeman," only the other word came out.

Sometimes, of course, you have to really put your thinking cap on. You may feel as though you're playing a combination of charades and twenty questions. Before my mother began speaking enough for us to understand a great deal of what she was trying to communicate, she regained her ability to write a little. Unfortunately what she wrote wasn't always what her mind was thinking, or if it was, it was in an abbreviated form that made us feel we were playing a bizarre word game. Luckily, I was always good at word games.

One day she wrote, "Bary Redkin." I looked at the notepad. I have a nephew Barry, but his last name is not Redkin. I let my mind wander, trying to solve the puzzle. What about my nephew tied into the second word? Suddenly I had the answer. He went to school at American University, which is in Washington, D.C. The Redskins play football there. "Is Barry going to the Redskins game?" I asked.

Mother nodded happily. We had communicated. We both felt good. Unfortunately our word games weren't always as successful. In fact, in the beginning she usually ended up feeling frustrated, while the rest of us felt stupid for not being able to figure out what she was trying to tell us. We all felt exhausted with the effort.

Never kid yourself. Trying to understand your family member's speech is exhausting work. No matter how much you love them and want to be supportive, it is every bit as fatiguing as hard physical labor. You may feel like screaming; you may feel like sobbing. Knowing that the person you love is frustrated too doesn't make it any easier.

When I asked my brother what message he thought was most important to stress in this book, he answered without hesitation. "Patience," he said. "It takes so much patience. I had no idea how hard this waiting would be on us all."

9

Coping with the Physical Aftereffects of Stroke

Just as a stroke can damage or destroy the part of the brain that controls speech, it also can wreak havoc on muscular control, thereby having the potential to alter much of a person's former way of life. As mentioned previously, if the stroke injures the left side, or hemisphere, of the brain, there is paralysis, called hemiplegia, of some degree on the right side of the body. If it damages brain cells on the right side, the resulting paralysis will be on the left side of the body.

Severity of Paralysis May Vary

There is a wide range in the degree of paralysis that may follow a stroke, ranging from most severe—total paralysis, difficulty in breathing and swallowing—to a slight numbness of one side of the face or fingers. Most stroke patients fall somewhere in between.

In addition, your relative may have paralysis on one side immediately after the stroke, only to have it dissipate over the following months until it stabilizes as a muscle weakness; it may even vanish entirely, leaving only a slight drooping of one side of the mouth or a numb or tingling feeling of the fingers. Physical therapy—and time, a great deal of time—plays an important part in this improvement.

It's difficult to understand the stress and frustration ex-

137

perienced by the stroke patient who must relearn basic functions like walking or self-feeding, unless you've been there yourself. About eight years ago I had surgery on my left hand, my dominant one. Although I had no pain, I found myself exhausted and often close to tears as I tried to accomplish the most basic tasks, such as brushing my teeth, zipping my slacks, signing a check, or cutting food, all with only my right hand. Try these activities with your nondominant hand and you'll understand.

Learning to master the functioning of the nondominant hand, however, is only one of the many challenges facing a patient whose stroke weakened or paralyzed one side. Walking, transferring (moving from the bed to the wheelchair, wheelchair to a car, and so on), self-feeding, bowel training, and dressing are just a few of the others. Physical impairments take many forms, and difficulties in one area may impact upon others. In addition, the therapy required to overcome the problems are tiring, seemingly endless, and at times, even painful.

Early Physical Therapy

When you visit your family member in the acute care hospital, you may be surprised to see a physical therapist working with him just a few days after the stroke. She may gently lift and turn his foot or raise his arm if he is not able to do so. This is done to prevent a number of potential problems.

Bed Sores

Also known as a decubitus ulcer or pressure sore, this condition is caused by poor blood circulation, triggered by a lack of mobility and a lack of sensation. Most of us shift position often as we sit on a chair or lie in bed. If we've been sitting a long time, at a boring meeting or dull lecture, we may actually begin to squirm. But after a stroke, a person may be physically unable to move as well as having no sensation of pressure on a particular area of his body. The pressure builds up, especially over the bony parts of the body—sacrum (the last bone of the spine, an area directly above the buttocks), elbow, heel, and so on, stopping circulation to the area and ending in breakdown of the skin. The resulting ulcers may cause skin irritations, or they may go deep into underlying tissue and cause serious damage.

To prevent bedsores, nurses will reposition a bedridden patient every two hours. The physical therapist also helps by conducting passive range-of-motion exercises, and if the stroke patient is able to cooperate, she helps him perform gentle exercises as well.

If your family member remains bedridden or must spend much time in a wheelchair once you get him home, you need to continue to move his position, check his skin often for potential pressure sores, keep his skin clean and dry, check the bedclothes for crumbs that can irritate delicate skin, and seek medical attention at the first sign of a problem. Bedsores can be a serious condition.

Blood Clots

Blood clots may form in the leg veins when someone is bedridden. Range-of-motion exercises speed up circulation and prevent these dangerous clots from forming. That's also why you'll find your family member sitting up on a chair at the hospital as soon after the stroke as the doctor says it is permissible.

Contractures

You probably have seen stroke survivors who have one arm pulled up across their chest like a wounded paw. This deformity is caused by a shortening or contracting of the muscle that bends the arm, which thus forces the arm firmly into that position.

In addition to performing range-of-motion exercises to prevent the muscle from contracting, the physical therapist may suggest the use of a splint. You and other members of your family should observe and learn how to safely perform the range-of-motion exercises, in case you need to continue with them once the stroke survivor is released from the hospital. Never try to help with these exercises without being properly trained by the therapist. You could cause damage.

Flaccidity

This is a condition created when the stroke has paralyzed a person's limb. You'll notice the physician lifting your relative's arm, then releasing it. The arm may drop as though weighted, falling down to the bedclothes. The degree of flaccidity can vary. Some people have no movement at all; others may have slight movement. The condition need not be permanent. Although my mother's right arm was flaccid for a few days after the stroke, she regained full use of it in less than a month.

If you've ever lifted a sleeping child or had to pick up a small pet after it was hit by a car, you'll know how heavy "dead weight" can be. If there is no muscle tone at all in the patient's upper arm, its weight can actually pull the arm out of the shoulder joint. A sling is often used to help support the weight of the flaccid limb.

Walking

The ability to walk again after a stroke is often regained, but usually not without a great deal of time and painful effort. Just as a baby usually begins by crawling, then pulling himself up, and finally taking a first tottering step, a stroke survivor usually begins his way back by first strengthening his muscles, then standing between parallel bars, held firmly by the therapist, who talks him through the walking process.

It doesn't come easily, this relearning business. The stroke survivor must think constantly about what he is doing as he lifts one leg, then puts it down, reminding his brain to redirect instructions to the legs. It takes great concentration. When you watch the therapist working with your family member, you'll see how intense a labor it is. There's no background music to distract, no side conversation. It's important to remember when your loved one comes home and you're the one offering physical and emotional support.

Motor Apraxia

If the stroke survivor has motor apraxia, he will be able to stand up or step out automatically, but if you say "Stand up" or "Take a step," he will look at you in confusion. Don't assume he is being contrary and just won't follow instructions. The problem is, he *can't* follow them. He may understand you but just cannot initiate the movement. The stroke has damaged the control center that tells the muscles to move in order to stand. He can stand, step out, wave, or do other spontaneous movements, but not on command. He also could be suffering from receptive dysphasia, so he does not understand what he is being asked to do.

Balance Deficit

Many stroke survivors have difficulty walking because they keep losing their balance. This may be due to

1. weakness or paralysis on one side of the body;
2. damage to the part of the brain that controls balance;
3. visual problems, such as double vision or blind spots;
4. environmental hazards, such as noise distraction, uneven surfaces caused by thick carpet or cobblestone walks, or toys or pets underfoot;
5. fear of falling;
6. lack of body awareness.

Walking Tips

Although the stroke survivor begins to walk between the parallel bars, hopefully she soon progresses to a wider world. She may need the aid of a walker or a three- or four-prong cane. Be sure to get one that is adjustable for height or bring the stroke patient to a hospital supply store so she can be fitted properly.

Those with impaired walking ability often are stymied by stairs. You can help by remembering this rhyme:

You can climb stairs without going mad,
Up with the good; and down with the bad.

What that ditty means is that the stroke patient should lead with her good or nonimpaired leg when going up the steps. When coming down, she should lead with the weak leg, holding on to the banister for security as she slowly goes down the stairs. You and other family members may need to remind the stroke patient which leg to step up with until it becomes almost second nature.

Don't grab the stroke survivor when offering support. Your sudden movement may throw her off balance. If she has visual or sensory deficits, she may not sense you on her "bad" side. Instead, slowly come up to her unimpaired side and gently take her arm or hand. That way you can guide her away from obstacles and offer support at the same time. Move slowly so she doesn't feel rushed.

Visual Difficulties

A stroke can cause a number of visual problems as well.

Visual Inattention

People with right-brain strokes may suffer from visual inattention, which means they do not see or even sense things on their left side. They may begin reading in the center of the page, totally omitting what's written on the left-hand side. A man may only shave the right side of his face; a woman may brush only the right side of her hair. Even more seriously, a stroke survivor with visual inattention may walk into a wall or door or may push his wheelchair into something because he did not see it on his impaired side. You need to remind him to turn his head to compensate for this visual deficit.

Hemianopsia

This visual problem is caused by damage to the brain cells that serve the optic nerve. Vision in the same half of each eye is affected, causing blindness in the stroke survivor's field of vision. Although therapy cannot cure hemianopsia, it can teach the patient to move his head so he can see everything on his plate or an entire page.

Corrective lenses or eyeglasses will *not* correct hemianopsia because. it is not the eye that needs strengthening; the damage is to the brain cells that give impulses to the optic nerve.

Double Vision

Some stroke patients, often those who have had a brain stem stroke, also suffer from double vision, so that they see double images. Fortunately, this troublesome symptom often disappears during the early stages of recovery.

Nystagmus

Brain stem strokes often cause a problem called nystagmus, in which the patient's eyeballs move constantly and rhythmically, either in a horizontal or vertical motion. Patients are seldom aware of nystagmus and it does not impair focus.

Preexisting Conditions

Preexisting illnesses, such as diabetes, can create additional problems, in the form of blurred vision or even blindness. Many elderly stroke survivors also may suffer from cataracts, which blur vision as well.

Swallowing Problems

Dysphagia, or difficulty in swallowing, may be present in the stroke survivor for a number of reasons:

1. There may be a numbness or sensory deficit in the mouth, tongue, cheek, and throat so that the patient doesn't sense where food or liquid actually is or feel differences in texture.
2. There may be dysarthria, or a weakness in the voice-

producing muscles, which in turn may prevent the swallowing reflex from functioning.

3. There may be other nonstroke-related factors such as poor-fitting dentures, fear, fatigue, depression, enlarged heart (which presses against the esophagus), progressive diseases like multiple sclerosis or Lou Gehrig's disease (amyotrophic lateral sclerosis), or gastrointestinal disorders.

In addition to being observed and tested by the speech therapist and physician, the doctor often will order barium X-rays to determine the severity of the swallowing difficulty, whether or not the patient can swallow sitting up, and what types of liquids and different food textures can and cannot be swallowed.

Interestingly, according to Dr. Bruce B. Grynbaum, clinical director and vice-chairman of the Howard A. Rusk Institute of Rehabilitation Medicine, NYU Medical Center, the most difficult substance to swallow is water and other clear liquids. Many stroke survivors who choke on thin liquids are able to comfortably swallow liquids with some texture, such as milk shakes, nectars, and unjelled Jell-O.

According to Marion C. Kagel, M.A., CCC-SLP/L, founder and director of the Swallowing Clinic at the Crozer-Chester Medical Center near Philadelphia, "Some patients with right-brain CVAs aren't even aware that they have a swallowing deficit. As this type of patient tends to be impulsive and have sensory deficits, they may actually shovel in mouthful after mouthful of food and not feel it or be aware that they are choking."

In the past fifteen years a number of comprehensive "swallowing clinics" have been established around the country to help diagnose and treat swallowing disorders. In addition to working with the stroke survivor, they also teach swallowing techniques to family members, speech-language pathologists interested in specializing in dysphagia, and others who deal with the patient. A few of these specialized centers are located at:

The Crozer-Chester Medical Center, Medical Center Blvd., Upland, Pennsylvania 19013, (215) 447-2000

University of South Florida Swallowing Center, 12901 Bruce B. Downes Blvd., MDC Box 72, Tampa, Florida 33612, (813) 974-3374

Johns Hopkins Medical Institution, 600 N. Wolfe St., Baltimore, Maryland 21205

New York Hospital-Cornell Medical Center, 525 E. 68th St., New York, New York 10021, (212) 746-5454

Most major hospital stroke rehabilitation programs, however, with multidiscipline teams of gastroenterologists, neurologists, speech-language pathologists trained in dealing with dysphagia, radiologists, and psychologists can help stroke survivors who suffer from swallowing problems. The goal, according to Ms. Kagel, is to try to retrain the stroke survivor to swallow without choking or aspirating food or liquids into his lungs, in order to wean him, if possible, from the necessity of tube or IV feedings with their inherent medical problems.

Drooling

Of all the indignities suffered by a stroke survivor, one of the most humiliating is drooling. It's caused by a lack of feeling in the mouth. For most of us, when saliva gathers in our mouth, we sense it and swallow. But the stroke damages the sensory centers in the mouth and throat. The stroke survivor can't sense that the saliva is building up, and rather than being swallowed automatically, it dribbles down his chin. It's awkward for family and friends, but it's humiliating and demoralizing for the stroke survivor at a time when his self-image is already at an all-time low.

Encourage the stroke survivor to carry a handkerchief with him at all times and to pat his mouth with it on a regular basis. If he watches television, place signs by the screen that read, ''Swallow,'' or if he cannot read, put up a picture of a person's face as a reminder. Establish a secret signal, such as touching your mouth, to give a visual cue if you're out in public. Sweaters and other knit materials are less likely to show stains from drooling than silks or polyester cottons.

Eating Difficulties

Mealtime can quickly become one of the most emotional periods of the day when you're caring for a stroke patient. In addition to the physical problems created by the stroke—difficulties in swallowing, inability to self-feed, inability to see what's on one-half of the plate, and inability to feel what's in the mouth—the stroke patient also has a number of emotional problems to deal with at mealtime.

As you'll learn in a later chapter, most stroke survivors suffer from depression. It's certainly an appropriate response, since they have suffered a great many losses because of their stroke—independence, self-esteem, and job security, to name a few—but it is also a physical response caused by the trauma their body has experienced. Depression for whatever reasons can cause loss of appetite. It becomes a vicious circle. It's physically hard for the stroke survivor to eat and that depresses him, and he's depressed so he doesn't feel like eating anyway.

Create a Cheery Atmosphere for This Reluctant Diner

Use brightly colored terrycloth hand towels as napkins, so he can wipe his mouth often. When one side of the mouth is numb or paralyzed, the stroke patient may not be aware that he is drooling or that food is on the unfeeling side of his face. Show him how to pat his mouth after every few bites to check for food pockets.

Use a bath-size towel to cover the shirt area and prevent food from soiling his clothes.

Use a pretty plate with sides so the food won't fall off the edge of the plate as he tries to scoop it up. He may be using his nondominant hand or just trying to force noncomplying muscles into remembering how they worked prestroke. It's hard work, and it's s-l-o-w.

Minimize Distractions

Don't talk while he's trying to eat. He needs to concentrate on one thing at a time; if he's thinking about lifting a spoon or fork to his mouth, he can't focus on your words, too.

Limit "background noise." Many of us normally have the radio or television on in the background. After a while *we* may not even notice it, but it can jam the stroke survivor's circuits so that he is physically unable to concentrate on eating.

Don't get the stroke patient to the table until the food is ready to serve. Stroke survivors tend to have short attention spans. If he has to wait, he may lose interest, think he's already eaten, or become so impatient that he is unable to eat once the food does come.

To prevent sudden spills from drinking glasses being knocked over, use flat-bottomed glasses rather than those with a stem. A person with a right-brain injury tends to show impulsive behavior and have difficulty judging distances. Visual deficits also can cause water goblets to be toppled, which is embarrassing and upsetting for the stroke patient.

Because of the extreme effort expended in trying to eat, many stroke survivors feel exhausted afterward and are ready for a nap. Try to spend this time relaxing as well, rather than trying to get caught up in everything else that must be done. It will still be there after you've rested, but you may feel more like tackling it then.

Don't Offer Too Much Help

As frustrating as it may be to sit back and watch your loved one struggling, you must. Most of us err by offering too much help rather than not enough. Eventually the patient will just give up and give in, thus losing whatever gains have been made and any hope of becoming more independent. If the stroke survivor is able to feed himself, let him. It may take four times longer, but he needs this practice, independence, and sense of accomplishment. You can break or cut things into bite-size pieces, but unless he gives up or seems too exhausted or frustrated, don't feed him.

If you become impatient or upset sitting and watching your relative struggling to eat, move out of his sight so you don't distract him. Ask someone else to spell you at mealtimes. Young people often are very good at this chore, perhaps because they're not so far removed from learning how to eat themselves.

Some youngsters, however, become extremely distressed seeing an adult struggling to eat, spilling on themselves or not being aware that they are drooling. A thirty-year-old nurse said, "My grandmother lived with us for twenty years after her stroke. Although it didn't bother me when just our family was present, I hated to have my friends over for dinner because of her. I was, quite frankly, embarrassed about my grandmother's eating habits, even though I knew she couldn't help it. It never occurred to my mother to feed Gran first or to talk to us kids about what a struggle it was for her to learn to feed herself. We never discussed how I felt. I just stopped inviting people over for dinner. I wish I had been more tolerant, but I wasn't."

Encourage Adequate Liquid Intake

Adequate liquid intake—about six to eight 8-ounce glasses daily—is important to keep the stroke survivor from becoming dehydrated. It can also help with important bowel training because it prevents constipation. Always check with the patient's doctor first, however, as in some cases the physician will limit liquid intake to prevent specific medications and chemicals from being flushed out of the system.

Some patients have difficulty swallowing or, because of muscle weakness, keeping their lips together so the liquid stays in their mouth. Drinking straws may help. Thickened liquids such as nectars, milk shakes, or cream soups also may be easier to swallow than water or clear liquids.

Check for Food Pockets

Normally, when we have food in our mouth we feel it and either swallow or, if it's jammed between the teeth and gum, run our tongue over the food to dislodge it. It's more difficult for the stroke survivor who has a slight paralysis or loss of feeling on one side of the face. Food can pile up on one side until the person begins to resemble a hamster with one side of the mouth bulging with food.

Tell your family member when you notice this food buildup and encourage him to run his tongue (if it's not too weak) or finger between the teeth and the gum to dislodge the food so he doesn't choke. You can develop a signal between you in order to avoid embarrassment to the stroke patient. Either tap the side of your cheek, say, "Cheek," or use some different sign. He can mask this action with his napkin if he's able to use both of his hands.

Bowel and Bladder Difficulties

One of the greatest indignities created by the stroke is loss of bowel and bladder control. For many stroke survivors, this is the ultimate humiliation. "Not only was I physically as helpless as a baby," a former business executive admitted, "but I had no speech and, like a baby, wet myself. That was my lowest point." Fortunately, in all but the most serious cases, bowel and bladder problems usually clear up with proper retraining and time.

Although your family member may have a catheter to drain urine from the bladder immediately after a stroke, the stroke team's goal is to retrain normal bladder and bowel habits as soon as possible. This is begun by the hospital staff even before the patient becomes ambulatory.

Constipation

Constipation often is a common complaint after a stroke because of:

- the patient's relative inactivity
- lack of sensory awareness for the need to evacuate
- weakness in the muscles used to move the bowels
- inability to ask for the bedpan, commode, or toilet

Adequate liquid intake, fruits and vegetables, and other foods with fiber such as cereals, whole-grain breads, and bran can help soften and regulate the bowels. In some cases a bulking agent, such as Metamucil, is helpful. Never use commercial laxatives without a doctor's approval. A regular toilet routine, usually right after eating, is also helpful.

A stroke survivor requiring a wheelchair will be taught to "transfer," which means moving himself from the wheelchair to the toilet. Hospital aid stores and specialized catalogs offer devices to raise the height of the toilet seat to make transferring easier. If your bathroom is too small to accommodate a wheelchair and cannot be easily remodeled, ask the therapist about the availability and use of a commode chair. Offer privacy whenever possible to protect the stroke survivor's dignity.

Bladder Training

Many stroke survivors initially suffer from incontinence (the inability to hold their urine). They may not feel the need to void, may not remember how or be able to express their need to go, or may just wait too long. For those who are aware of what's happened, an "accident" is humiliating for the patient and upsetting for the family, who are embarrassed for their loved one. Retraining a stroke patient to control his or her bladder is a most important goal for many reasons, including:

- freeing the patient from requiring a catheter, thus reducing the possibility of infection
- permitting more mobility and independence
- reducing the risk of skin irritations
- promoting better self-image
- reinforcing the sense of "getting better"

Although your family member's therapist will tell you specifically how to work with your relative's problems of incontinence, consider taking the stroke survivor to the bathroom every few hours in the daytime and right before bedtime, just as you did when first toilet training a toddler. Restricting liquids at night also proves effective.

If there is a urinary accident, clean it up with a minimum of discussion to prevent embarrassment, but gently remind the patient to let you know his needs earlier next time. For stroke survivors requiring "adult diapers," be as matter-of-fact as you can when changing them. Refer to them as "pads" rather than diapers, to prevent your family member from feeling as though he really has slipped back into babyhood. *Remember, even though a patient doesn't seem to hear what you say, he may understand every word.* Protect your loved one's feelings and his shaky self-esteem at all times.

Bathing

What formerly was a relatively simple task—bathing—often becomes a production for the stroke survivor. Tub baths are complicated by many stroke-related problems. Paralysis on one side makes climbing into and out of the tub precarious. Numbness and loss of sensory perception on one side also makes water temperature a potential hazard. In addition, the stroke survivor may have difficulty maintaining balance.

Although a shower has the advantage of allowing the stroke survivor to sit on a shower chair through the procedure, it too has its shares of possible problems, including loss of balance, loss of vision from steam buildup, and danger from turning the wrong faucet when water is in the eyes.

Most experts encourage the use of a tub seat, which is a plastic seat that sits firmly in the bottom of the tub. It raises the stroke patient and makes it easier for him to climb in and out and to transfer from the wheelchair; if your help is needed, a tub seat makes it easier for you to ease the person out. Be sure to learn the safe way to help move your family member so you don't injure your back. Always lift by bending your knees, not your back.

A stroke patient could lose his balance trying to juggle slippery soap. Using "soap on a rope" keeps the soap handy, so neither you nor the bather have to bend to grope for it. A hand-held shower attachment makes rinsing and hair washing easier and safer.

Be sure to install grab bars for the tub, shower, and toilet area. Use only nonskid rugs in the bathroom and check them often. The rubberized backing often deteriorates after many washings and dryings.

Dressing and Grooming

If you've had small children, you know how frustrating it can be to see them dawdling over getting dressed. They stick their arms through the head holes, have part of the slacks inside-out, and become so fascinated studying a button or zipper that they forget they were supposed to get dressed.

Stroke patients may have many of the same difficulties. Concentration is difficult after a stroke. The patient may become easily distracted by a bird singing outside the window, a clock chiming, or a dog barking. Those suffering from agnosia may not remember what a blouse is for or where pants belong. They may have extreme weakness on one side, be paralyzed on one side (hemiplegia), or have no sensory awareness of one side. All these problems make the once simple act of dressing most difficult.

Encourage Getting Dressed

It's often easier for everyone—you and the stroke survivor—to just let her stay in her robe and gown. But she needs to get dressed. It's important for many reasons:

- improves self-image
- signifies "getting well"

- various movements strengthen muscles
- boosts independence

You may meet with some resistance when you insist on your family member's getting dressed. Be firm.

Make Dressing as Easy as Possible

Remember your experiences trying to dress yourself with one hand? It's not easy. Resist the temptation to do it yourself, but help your loved one dress himself by adapting some of the following tips suggested by those who have been there:

- When dressing, put clothes on the weakest limb first.
- When undressing, take clothes off the strongest limb first.
- Use elastic waistbands whenever possible.
- Wherever possible, use Velcro instead of buttons or zippers.
- Wear shoes with Velcro fasteners or elastic shoelaces.
- Men who only have the use of one hand can wear clip-on ties.
- Women who only have the use of one hand can wear clip-on earrings.
- Dress sitting down.

If you have any questions about ways in which your family member can dress himself more easily, contact the occupational therapist of your nearest stroke club or stroke rehabilitation unit. Members of a stroke club also are good sources for suggestions. In addition, there are mail-order houses, such as Comfortably Yours, that stock numerous dressing, grooming, and bathing aids. Write for a catalog:

Comfortably Yours
2515 E. 43rd St.
Chattanooga, TN 37422
(615) 867-9977

When to Lend a Hand

It's extremely difficult to know when to stand back and let the stroke survivor learn to do his or her own ADLs (activities of daily living). With training and persistence, and encouragement from the family, many stroke patients can become quite self-sufficient.

There are times, however, when careful observation will make you aware that your help is needed. Your family member may be frustrated with a task and just give up, or he may struggle and not want to admit that he can't do it alone.

As each stroke situation is unique, each family must discover for themselves where a gentle helping hand is needed. You might be needed to

trim a mustache

My father has worn a mustache since he was a young man in his twenties. As children, my sister and I used to drive him crazy by stealing his special mustache scissors to cut out our paper dolls. Now I'm paying him back. I asked a barber for a quick lesson in mustache trimming and once or twice a month trim his mustache so it doesn't droop. He seems pleased, although no one else in the nursing home has asked for my services.

help with shaving

Although rehabilitation usually teaches men to shave with an electric razor, those with severe paralysis or limited range of motion in their unaffected arm may need your help. Both men and women who have sufficient arm movement can use battery-operated razors to prevent possible shock.

give a manicure and/or pedicure

It's hard enough to file and polish the nails on your dominant hand when you haven't had a stroke. The stroke survivor may find the fine muscle control manicures require difficult. Visual problems, lack of concentration, and numbness may further impede progress.

Also give attention to the stroke patient's feet. Sensory impairments may prevent him from feeling ingrown toenails until they become badly infected. Blisters, fungus infections, and other foot problems need to be treated early by a podiatrist, a specialist in disease and other problems of the human foot. Be especially watchful of the stroke patient's feet if he is also a diabetic.

Fatigue

Fatigue seems to be an ever-present problem for the stroke survivor and must be taken into consideration at all times, especially after physical exertion. Plan walks in areas where benches or other seating facilities are available. Schedule time for naps after a walk or therapy. Offer moments of "quiet time" after the stroke patient has been in a crowd, as the noise and stimulation from large groups can trigger distraction, anxiety, and general stress overload. Things we take for granted—speaking, eating, writing, and so on—require a tremendous effort on the part of the stroke survivor.

You may help your relative to transfer from bed into his wheelchair, only to have him want to return to bed just a few hours later. He's not playing games with you, being contrary, or trying to attract your attention. He's probably just plain tired. What we may take for withdrawal or disinterest often may be signs of fatigue. This reduced energy level often threatens a stroke survivor's chances to return to the work force. His speech may have improved and he may be able to get around with a cane or wheelchair, but he is just too exhausted with the effort needed for those accomplishments to have enough stamina left to get through a typical nine-to-five workday. Additionally, the stroke survivor usually has more difficulty in speaking or pronouncing words properly when he is fatigued. Part-time employment or flexible hours may need to be considered.

What about Driving?

Driving! The word conjures up images of power. In America the ability and license from one's state of residence to operate a motor vehicle is our "coming of age" ceremony. It is the threshold of adulthood.

What happens, then, to the stroke survivor, who fears losing this badge of responsibility? The vehicle's key to independence?

It becomes a most emotional issue. It's difficult enough when the family worries about Grandpa's driving because he's getting deaf or doesn't see so well. But when the driver in question is a recovering stroke patient, you don't want to upset or depress him any further. You hate to take away his wheels, his chance for independence. On the other hand, you worry if it's safe for him to drive.

We found it difficult to get a definite answer from anyone. The therapists said to "ask the doctor." The doctor said, "If she feels comfortable." My mother said, "No," and then later, "Yes."

Many rehabilitation centers test their patients in simulated driving conditions or on an actual private track. In some states a stroke survivor's insurance is not valid unless she has been tested by the state. Other states require letters of permission from the stroke survivor's physician before relicensing. Some states issue handicapped permits to stroke patients who may drive.

The dangers of driving after a stroke are obvious. If vision is impaired, the stroke survivor may not have sufficient peripheral vision or depth perception. She may have blind spots or double vision. Reaction time may be slower. Heavy traffic or hazardous driving conditions may distract or confuse her. Judgment may be faulty. If speech is a problem, stress and fear may prevent your relative from expressing herself if stopped by a police officer. You might type a card for her wallet that reads, "Because of a stroke, I often have difficulty in speaking. I *do*, however, understand everything you say."

Only a driving instructor who has had experience with stroke survivors can determine whether or not your relative should drive again. Don't just rationalize that, "well, Mother drives too slowly to get into trouble," or "Grandpa just drives to and from church." According to the National Safety Council, most accidents happen within five minutes

of home. It's too important a decision to leave up to chance.
Contact the rehabilitation center or the Easter Seal Society
for a list of names of professional driving instructors in your
area.

As with all residual effects of stroke, the physical impairments vary in degree and type depending on each individual. The physical therapist and occupational therapist at
your hospital stroke unit or rehabilitation center are the best
sources for information and suggestions on how to handle
your family member's particular set of problems.

There's no denying that it takes a great deal of time to
help a stroke survivor practice what he has learned in therapy. The day isn't long enough, especially if you have your
own job to do as well. But if you don't let him repeat what
he has learned, he'll never come any closer to independence
and you'll find yourself constantly overwhelmed and exhausted.

Regardless of how dedicated and loving you are, you're
not the only person who can work with your loved one,
assisting with meals, bathing, and the thousands of daily
details the professionals label "activities of daily living."
Even if you're the only relative in town, additional help is
available. If you don't read another chapter in this book,
read chapter 12.

10

Personality Changes and What to Do about Them

During the acute stage of your family member's stroke, you and the rest of the family are consumed by the shock and fear of the unknown. Your questions speak of your priorities. Will he live? Will he ever walk again? Will he be able to speak? What about his job?

If the stroke survivor's next step is the rehabilitation center, you again are focused on the various types of therapies and the vital part you and the rest of the family must play in reinforcing what your relative is learning in order to function again in the everyday world.

If you notice subtle changes in your loved one's personality, they probably don't register at first. Your attention is elsewhere. But soon, a casual comment made and then picked up by another in the family—"Yes, I've noticed that, too"—suddenly creates a stunning awareness that the stroke survivor's personality has changed.

Depression

One of the most universal responses among stroke survivors is that of depression. "I think depression is a most appropriate response," said Dr. Bruce B. Grynbaum, director of the Institute of Rehabilitation Medicine, NYU Medical Center. "The stroke survivor is mourning the loss of his or her prestroke life. The important questions are 'How severe is the depression?' and 'How long is it lasting?' People who were basically negative people before their stroke tend to be more depressed than those who were upbeat and optimistic in their view of the world.''

Some depression is not just reactive, the patient reacting to all his losses and frustration. A stroke inflicts horrible trauma to the brain, short-circuiting normal pathways, disrupting chemical and electrical flows to muscles and other organs, and damaging or destroying vital brain cells. It can trigger a chemically induced depression upon the stroke survivor. As the swelling recedes and the brain begins the long recovery process, depression may slowly lift. If not, the patient's doctor may need to treat the depression with antidepressants and other medications. If you are concerned about your family member's depression in any way, contact his doctor for advice.

According to Marion C. Kagel, M.A., CCC-SLP/L, administrative director of the Crozer-Chester Medical Center's Rehabilitation Department, stroke survivors go through many of the same stages attributed to those who are dying, as described by Dr. Elisabeth Kübler-Ross in her book *On Death and Dying.*[1] These stages, which don't necessarily follow in order, include denial and isolation, anger, bargaining, depression, and acceptance. Not surprisingly, family members of stroke survivors also experience these stages of response, which will be discussed in chapter 12.

Anger

Depression is anger turned inward. It isn't surprising that a stroke survivor is angry. His entire life has been turned inside-out. He may be paralyzed or have lost the use of one side of his body. His communication skills may be totally lost or reduced to primitive motions and gruntings. In min-

1. Elisabeth Kübler-Ross, *On Death and Dying* (New York: MacMillan Publishing Co., Inc., 1969).

utes he found himself transformed from a self-confident and independent, functioning adult into an always fatigued and often bewildered individual who requires help for the most basic needs and is alternatingly ignored or treated like a foolish child.

"I felt as though I had been buried alive," a stroke survivor confided, weeping anew at the memory of an experience more than two years in her past. "I was screaming inside, but no one heard. It was my worst nightmare come true. I was locked inside myself."

But it's not just the stroke survivor who feels anger at the blow he has suffered. Family members also share this emotion. A loved one's stroke affects everyone. I personally recall feeling intense anger after receiving word that my mother had suffered a stroke. "Why?" I asked my husband. "It's not fair. She has only just begun to pick up the pieces after Daddy's stroke." That unresolved anger remained with me for many months. Chapter 12 details ways in which you can resolve or best handle this potentially destructive emotion.

Expressing anger is difficult for many stroke patients. Often unable to satisfactorily vent their anger verbally or unwilling to rail against therapists, nurses, or doctors, they may lash out at you, either verbally or physically. As overwhelming as this response may be, try to remain calm but firm. Tell your family member that you understand his fury, but that you won't allow him to strike you or be verbally abusive. Acknowledge his feelings, then try to distract him with something more positive, either visually, by changing his environment (moving his wheelchair to a window or different view of the house); verbally, by complimenting his appearance or recent progress; or tactually, by rubbing his neck and shoulders or gently massaging his hands and fingers.

I have found massage to be the most successful way to dispel my father's frequent angry outbursts. I gently rub lotion into his hands and fingers, which gives his dry skin much-needed moisture. The massage improves his circulation, and the gentle pulling of his fingers seems to relax him. A welcomed side effect is that I find his massage to be soothing to me as well. We communicate, without words, through touch. Never underestimate the power of "the laying on of hands."

Although anger is triggered by frustration and depression, some of the stroke survivor's anger also may be caused by the actual trauma and damage to the brain. But even though you understand that the stroke patient may not realize what he is saying and have empathy for his extreme frustration, you may still feel terribly hurt when he shouts at you to go away, throws things, strikes out with his cane, curses, or waves you away with one hand. It's hard not to take it personally, even though you know intellectually that you shouldn't. Chapter 12 describes ways to express your feelings so you don't keep them locked inside you like some dreaded secret. You're not the only person whose loved one's personality changed after a stroke. We've all been shocked at the transformation; we've all cried into our pillows; we've all thought, "Maybe it's just me."

It isn't.

Loss of Self-Esteem

Most stroke survivors acutely feel and mourn their loss of control over their lives. Ironically, the stroke often destroys that which once brought the most pride and satisfaction to the individual. Thus the writer loses her ability to craft characters and scrawl sentences from thin air; the surgeon loses the gift of guiding scalpel through living tissue and now struggles merely to hold on to his spoon or remember where his bedroom is located; the politician is mute; the banker can no longer count; the homemaker feels helpless in her own home.

We are what we do, society tells us. For the stroke survivor who can no longer do, what is there? Eventually, of course, occupational therapy retrains and helps the patient at least to find some direction, if not head back. But while all that goes on, life continues as well. The stroke survivor must discover what he is along the way and what can give him pride and self-esteem at the present.

His family also must readjust to his new identity and accept him on that level. It no longer may be "Dad, the carpenter, who can do anything with his hands," but "Dad, the carpenter, who can tell us how to fix it," or even "who taught us how to fix it." Self-esteem is a lot like good health; you don't think about it until it's gone.

Give your family member whatever control of his life you can. Mark the calendar so he knows what day he has therapy; show him two shirts and let him select what shirt to wear. Don't offer too many choices, however, and don't be surprised if he is unable to make a decision.

For some families, a loved one's stroke shakes their own self-esteem as well. There may be financial difficulties now and a loss of social prestige. A woman who felt confident with her identity as "Mr. Important's wife" may feel lost if, after her husband's stroke, she suddenly must become the provider, the plan maker, the dominant one. By the same token, a man whose wife has had a stroke may feel a tremendous emptiness now that his wife is ill and he must give her emotional support *and* help run the house, do errands, care for the children, and the like.

Isolation

"Having a stroke is like waking up and finding yourself on a desert island," said a middle-aged former writer. "You're cut off from everybody."

This sense of isolation permeated most of my interviews with stroke survivors and families alike. Although they understood people's feeling of uncertainty over how to behave around a stroke patient, they felt hurt at being left out. It tended to be worse among those suffering from aphasia.

"I know I speak slowly, and you can't always understand me," an elderly woman said, "but if they'd take the time to listen, I *can* communicate. And I can hear," she continued. "People ask my daughter how I'm doing and I'm sitting right there. When my daughter says, 'Ask *her*,' and points to me, they look embarrassed."

"My husband is bedridden," a frail woman confided in a soft whisper, "but I'm not. I wish someone would ask me to join them for dinner or a movie. Our friends come over to visit from time to time, but no one ever thinks I might like to get out of the house. I would. Is that awful of me?"

"A couple of our friends said they'd like to invite us to dinner and the theater, but knew it would be such a hassle with Tony's wheelchair," a New York lawyer said. "I assured them that his chair could fold up and go into the trunk of a cab. Then they stuttered something about the restaurant being up some stairs and no elevator. I may be too sensitive, but it certainly seemed that they didn't want to be bothered with dealing with Tony's limitations. He spills a little when he eats, and he's changed. He's rude and far more argumentative since his stroke. But he's still Tony, their friend. At least he was. Now they act like he's someone else. It hurts us both."

Most of the people telling these anecdotes never bothered to tell their friends how much it hurt. They just accepted the isolation and, along with the stroke survivor, fell into a depression. Those who finally did speak out were surprised at the response. Often their friends had left them alone because they didn't know how to respond—"What should we do when we can't understand what the stroke survivor is saying? What should we say or do when our friend spills food or has some on the side of his face but, because of the paralysis, doesn't feel? Should we take his arm to help him walk? What if he starts yelling at us?"

Encourage—urge, if necessary—the stroke survivor's friends to visit or join you and your family member for an evening out. Tell them you know they may have questions

that, perhaps, you can answer. Offer suggestions based on
how you handle specific problems. If the stroke patient has
fits of anger or is rude, tell them how you respond. Admit
that your loved one is depressed, that he feels lonely and
left out. Often, when friends know what to do and that they
can help, they will.

Emotional Lability

It's difficult to cope with your relative's sudden, inexpli-
cable outbursts, even when you know it is caused by brain
damage and that he can't help it. But there are other emotional responses that are equally mystifying. Emotional lability is a strange phenomenon in which the stroke survivor
begins to laugh or cry for no apparent reason. It is a bit
startling the first time you see it.

For my interviews for this book, I met with a number of
stroke survivors in a variety of settings. My meeting with a
theater personality who was a stroke survivor took place in
his favorite restaurant. As soon as I sat down, he warned
me, "I have two main residual effects from my stroke. My
left leg is weak, and I have a low threshold for tears and
laughter."

I nodded and proceeded with my questions. As I paused
to write a note, I was amazed to see tears running down his
face. He was sobbing softly. Then it grew louder. I quickly
tried to reconstruct what we had been saying, thinking that
I had upset him in some way. Then I remembered. He was
displaying emotional lability. I waited for it to end, which
it did rather quickly, and we continued with the interview.
It hadn't attracted any notice in the noisy restaurant, but
imagine the effect if he had begun to sob at a dinner party
or at a play. Uncontrollable crying especially tends to upset
families of those who, prior to their stroke, were not partic-
ularly emotional.

The opposite emotion, that of uncontrollable laughter,
can also occur and can create quite a stir among those who

don't understand what is happening, especially if it happens at a church service, a concert, or at a meeting. These inappropriate emotions may go away in time. Until that happens, however, you might want to warn friends and other relatives to try to ignore emotional lability when it occurs. Some therapists teach the stroke survivor distraction techniques, so that when he begins to laugh or cry inappropriately, he learns to grip the arms of the wheelchair. This action tends to interrupt the impulse that causes the emotional lability. You also can cough, clap your hands, snap your fingers, or ask a question to distract him.

Sexuality

When I was thirty, I had my gall bladder removed. My recovery was normal. The day I was to be released from the hospital, my surgeon came to see if I had any questions.

"Just one," I said. "When can we resume sexual relations?" My physician blushed, stammered, joked about what a lucky man my husband was, and fled.

Although that was more than twenty years ago, some things never change. Numerous spouses told me they received no information whatsoever from their doctors concerning sexual relations, such as whether it was "safe" to resume marital relations, how to practice birth control, and possible problems or suggestions. If it was discussed at all, they said, it usually was brought up by one of the nurses on the rehabilitation team.

If no one on the stroke team has mentioned this issue to you and your spouse, initiate the discussion. If the physician seems uncomfortable with the topic, ask to speak with someone else.

You're Never "Too Old"

The myth that "old people don't 'do it' " dies hard. Yet frequently even medical professionals feed into it, by assuming that whoever is "old" by that particular doctor's standards is no longer interested in sex. Stroke patients who are residents of nursing homes also housing their mates often find themselves separated from their spouses and given no opportunity even for private cuddling.

At home, families may without thinking set up the patient's bedroom in a high-traffic area or one offering little privacy, not realizing that it destroys any chance for intimacy. Even if a couple doesn't want to have sexual intercourse, they still need privacy for hugging, kissing, and other mutual forms of sexual satisfaction. Sex *is* important for those who desire it. It adds a sense of normalcy to the couple's life and offers hope for additional recovery.

What Causes Poststroke Sexual Problems?

According to nurse therapist Kate Brennan of the Rehabilitation Institute of Chicago, there are several areas of potential problems following someone's stroke, such as

in the case of a spouse who is also caregiver

"It's sometimes difficult to desire intimacy when you've been caring for and cleaning up after the stroke survivor," said Ms. Brennan. The stroke survivor's personality may have changed significantly as well, so your sweet and caring lover has suddenly been transformed into a rude, short-tempered person with a short attention span. You also may be overly fatigued and just too filled with the responsibility of your nursing tasks to feel like making love.

fear

You may have been having sex just before the patient suffered the stroke and feel (unnecessarily so) guilty that your passion caused the stroke. One or both of you may worry that intercourse might trigger another stroke. Although this is unlikely, you need to seek reassurance from the patient's physician. Many of the stroke survivors and their spouses that I interviewed told me confidentially that they had not resumed sexual relations since the stroke for fear of causing another attack.

sexual dysfunction from medications

In some cases the medication given for hypertension, depression, or other conditions may cause impotency. Don't just accept this condition passively. If impotency is a problem, tell the physician. He or she may be able to prescribe another drug that won't trigger this distressing side effect.

sexual dysfunction from psychological causes

Some male stroke survivors are unable to have an erection because of psychological causes. They may feel like failures and "less manly" because they can no longer be the breadwinner and are dependent in many ways on their wives.

If your husband's physician can find no physical reason for his impotency, try to work with the underlying causes. Perhaps you need to give him more responsibility or ask his opinion on things. Dr. Santosh Lai, attending physician of the Rehabilitation Institute of Chicago and assistant professor of the Rehabilitation Department of Northwestern University, suggests showing your spouse the checkbook, even if you are now paying the bills and handling the finances. "Just asking, 'Is there anything else you want me to do?' or asking for additional advice or suggestions can give a sense of self-esteem back to a stroke survivor who feels very unneeded. It may be more time-consuming for you at a period when you have far too little time, but it does offer the patient a valuable feeling of control." It's all too easy to take the ball and run with it when it's handed to you. Sometimes you need to do a little backtracking for the "good of the team." We all need to feel needed.

physical problems

Loss of sexual desire following a stroke may be caused by some of the physical residual effects. Lack of feeling or paralysis on one side may make former familiar types of foreplay or positions difficult to resume. Surprisingly, a paralyzed limb may be sensitive, even registering pain, when touched. It also may jerk or flop as though it had a life of its own.

Because human beings are essentially creatures of habit, some couples stop making love when the old way isn't successful, rather than making adjustments, experimenting with other positions or other foreplay techniques. The nonstroke mate may feel as though he or she is taking advantage of the stroke survivor and feel guilty for wanting sex, while the stroke survivor, who already suffers from a loss of self-esteem, feels as though he or she is no longer sexually desirable. Usually neither partner brings up the subject, creating even more distance between them at a time when both need reassurance and support.

Rather than just abandoning your sexual relationship, try to initiate open discussion about these problems with your partner. Meanwhile there are, of course, other ways to maintain a close physical relationship, such as hugging, caressing, and old-fashioned necking.

If you feel awkward talking about these subjects, consider seeing a qualified marriage and family therapist, psychiatrist, or your rabbi, minister, or priest. There also is an association for professionals in the field of sex education and sex counseling called the American Association of Sex Educators, Counselors, and Therapists. They offer certification to professionals in that field. For the names of qualified sex therapists in your state, send a self-addressed, stamped #10 envelope (the long narrow kind) to

> AASECT
> Suite 1717
> 435 N. Michigan Avenue
> Chicago, Illinois 60611
> (312) 644-0828

Birth Control

In addition to needing the physician's assurance that resuming sexual relations is perfectly safe, couples of child-bearing age may need birth control advice following a stroke, as former methods may no longer be feasible. A female stroke survivor should definitely *not* resume taking birth control pills without the advice of her physician. If one arm is paralyzed, a woman may not be able to properly insert a diaphragm. A man with extreme weakness or paralysis in one arm may not be able to put on a condom.

Personality changes such as anger, frustration, and impatience may make the stroke survivor irresponsible about birth control procedures. If possible, you should take over that responsibility.

The Importance of Exercise— Yours and Theirs

You may feel like becoming a little hysterical over the title of this chapter. "Exercise? When do I have time to exercise with everything else that's piling up? I'm so over-committed now, I hardly have time to go to the bathroom!"

I know how you feel. There have been times I felt so exhausted and overloaded that I wanted to crawl into a cave, pull a boulder across the opening, and hide. Well-meaning friends try to console, saying, "God never gives you more than you can handle." To them I reply, "I think He's got me mixed up with the lady down the street."

Stress Can Make You Ill

Yet I cope as you do. Because we must; because we care and because we love the person who has suffered this cruel stroke. We want to do all we can, and often we become so involved in our loved one's illness and his numerous prob-lems that we lose ourselves completely. And that's not smart. It's not being loyal, heroic, or saintly. It's stupid because it's slow suicide. Study after study illustrates how stress, worry, and fatigue lower immunity and can make you more susceptible to illness. If you become ill, who will take care of the stroke survivor? Who will take care of you?

In 1967 Drs. Thomas H. Holmes and Richard H. Rahe, psychiatrists at the University of Washington Medical

School, devised a scale of stressful events—some good, like weddings or graduations, and some bad, like death, loss of job, and financial difficulties. According to their study, a person's vulnerability to illness could be predicted fairly accurately according to their rating on the Social Readjustment Rating Scale.[1]

Illustration G

The Social Readjustment Rating Scale

Rank	Event	Value	You
1	Death of a spouse	100	
2	Divorce	73	
3	Marital separation	65	
4	Jail term	63	
5	Death of a close family member	63	
6	Personal injury/severe illness	53	
7	Marriage	50	
8	Fired at work	47	
9	Marital reconciliation	45	
10	Retirement	45	
11	Change in health of close family member	44	
12	Pregnancy	40	
13	Sex difficulties	39	
14	Gain of a new family member	39	
15	Business readjustment	39	
16	Change in financial state	38	
17	Death of a close friend	37	
18	Change to different work or school major	36	
19	Change in number of arguments w/spouse	35	
20	Home mortgage over $30,000	31	
21	Loan foreclosures/stress of unpaid bills	30	

1. Thomas Holmes and Richard Rahe, "The Social Readjustment Rating Scale," *Journal of Psychosomatic Research* 11 (1967): 212–218.

22	Change in work/school responsibilities	29
23	Son/daughter leaving home	29
24	Trouble with in-laws	29
25	Outstanding personal achievement	28
26	Spouse begin or stop work	26
27	Begin or end school	26
28	Revision of personal habits	24
29	Trouble with boss or school instructors	23
30	Change in work or social hours	20
31	Change in residence	20
32	Change in schools	20
33	Change in recreation	19
34	Change in church activities	18
35	Change in school activities	18
36	Mortgage or loan less than $30,000	17
37	Change in sleeping habits	16
38	Change in number of family get-togethers	15
39	Change in eating habits	15
40	Vacation	13
41	Christmas	12
42	Minor violations of the law	11

Total:

(Note: This scale applies to events you experienced within the past year.)

Scoring

150–199   Mild chance of incurring some form of illness in the next year

200–299   Moderate risk of incurring some form of illness in the next year

300+   Very likely to suffer serious physical or emotional illness

If you study this list carefully, you'll notice at least twenty-one out of forty-two potential stress events may be experienced by those of us who have a family member who is a stroke survivor. That's a total of over five hundred points!

In addition, researchers Richard Lazarus, Ph.D., Anita

DeLongis, Ph.D., Susan Folkman, Ph.D., and others completed a study in 1987 while they were at the University of California at Berkeley that weighed the effects of what they call "hassles," those everyday "minor" irritations of life. They found that continual daily events such as those caused by too much responsibility and constant interruptions can adversely affect an individual, eventually creating even more stress than a single traumatic life event. Interestingly, these daily "hassles" are normal situations for families dealing with stroke.

Although we can't change many of the sources of tension that flood our lives following a loved one's stroke, we can do something about handling the stress in a more positive way.

Many of the men and women who care for family members after a stroke spoke proudly to me about the exercise program they developed in order to "save sanity."

"Be sure to say that I always hated exercise," a middle-aged woman told me cheerfully. "Before my husband's stroke, my only walking was through the shopping malls and at a snail's pace so I wouldn't miss anything in the windows. I never lifted anything heavier than my loaded fork. But after Ben's stroke, exercise kept me going. I now have more energy than I ever did, and I'm caring for him almost alone."

The Benefits of Exercise

Humans were meant to be active creatures. Our cave-dwelling ancestors ran and climbed to hunt their prey. Their nervous system aided them by shutting down the digestive system and increasing the heart rate, oxygen consumption, and blood pressure so they could react more quickly to close in for the kill, escape danger from hostile beasts or warlike neighboring clans, and cope with the forces of nature. Physiologist Walter B. Cannon termed this the "fight or flight" response for survival.

Although our caves are now condos, our nervous system

remains as it was before. Our bodies prepare for a state of readiness, but there's no enemy to fight. The tensions are there, but there's no release. Yet survival is still the issue.

Reduces Tension

Exercise offers a release from that tension. It actually triggers the production of certain chemicals that create a sense of relaxation and well-being, a natural and healthy form of tranquilizer. You'll not only feel less stressed, you'll sleep better.

Reduces Fatigue

You have good reason to feel fatigued when you're caring for someone who has suffered a stroke. First of all, it's hard work. You've got the right to be tired. It also is a tremendous sense of responsibility to have another adult dependent upon you. Loving that person doesn't lighten the load; sometimes it actually increases the pressure.

Fatigue can also be a form of depression. It's easy to become depressed when someone you love has had a stroke. Recovery seems to take forever; you may feel frustrated when you can't understand what he is trying to tell you or when he screams and curses you and you're doing your level best. It seems you're always cleaning up, clearing up, or making up. You hardly remember what life BTS (before the stroke) was like. Tired? You're not tired, you're exhausted.

"How can I exercise?" you cry. "I'm too tired to think!" But strange as it sounds, exercise, as long as it isn't overdone, actually reduces fatigue. It makes you feel more alert and promotes a sense of well-being.

Helps Control Weight

Almost every diet plan today incorporates some aspect of exercise into its program and for a very good reason. In order to lose weight and keep it off, exercise is a vital necessity. It boosts the metabolism, causing your body to burn calories faster.

Improves Self-Esteem

You may have been so busy caring for your family member and adjusting to the stress triggered by his stroke that you've stopped thinking about caring for yourself as well. Many caregivers admit that they no longer bother to fix nutritious meals for themselves but instead "just grab something." Women feel guilty "wasting time" at the beauty parlor, so they stop going. Both men and women admit it often has been months since they last bought themselves new clothes or did much to enhance their sense of feeling good about themselves.

Exercise, with all its other magical qualities, can help change this. When you exercise you firm up muscle tone, so you not only feel better, you also look better. You feel more like getting your hair done, having a manicure, buying a new shirt, or just treating yourself kindly. Don't become so immersed in improving the stroke patient's sense of self-esteem that you lose all sense of yours. You can help your loved one *more* if you care about yourself as well. You'll also be better able to help him physically.

What Is the "Best" Exercise?

Fortunately there is no one particular exercise that is best. It depends on what you enjoy doing so you'll keep doing it. My interviewees used a number of choices—indoor and out—including biking and/or stationary bikes, swimming, walking, race walking, running, racquetball, jumping rope, and basketball.

Some of them preferred "mindless" solitary exercise such as swimming laps or walking on a treadmill. "I let my mind go blank. It's so relaxing," said a sixty-year-old man whose wife was bedridden.

Others looked forward to companionship found in playing games such as basketball or racquetball or walking with a friend. "We don't talk much," one woman confided, "but I enjoy the company. I drink in the sights, sounds, and smells—healthy children playing, dogs barking, planes overhead, fresh tar being spread on the streets. It reminds me that there's a whole world outside the sickroom, outside my house where my poor husband sits, blankly staring into space, never speaking or acknowledging me. My walks make me feel alive. I guess they're good for me—physically—but I *know* they're good for my soul.''

In some countries walking and biking are still major forms of transportation. In America, however, walking and biking for the most part are considered forms of exercise and activities warranting instruction books to tell us how to proceed. That means a little more effort on our part, but it's worthwhile.

When Should You Exercise?

There's no special time that's right for everyone. We all have our own internal time clocks. You may have to do some experimenting until you discover your "right" time, when you best can fit exercise into your crazy schedule. Don't wait to *find* the time; you have to make the time.

I personally prefer exercising the first thing in the morning. If I don't get on the treadmill by eight A.M., chances are that I won't bother exercising that day. I am not a lover of exercise, but I like having exercised. I feel better, my muscles feel less tense (I especially notice my face muscles relaxing), and I feel better able to handle (and dodge) what comes my way.

Don't feel that it is self-serving to ask a friend to stay with the patient so you can take an hour off for a run or dance class. It's good insurance. If you just can't bring yourself to do that on a regular basis, look into borrowing or renting (before buying) a stationary bike, cross-country ski machine, or rowing machine so you can exercise without leaving the house. If you can't justify the expense of equipment, get a jump rope or do aerobics in front of the television. You need that physical release of tension.

There's no doubt that regular exercise is important for your physical health as well as your mental health. In addition to helping with weight reduction, exercise helps to lower blood pressure and cholesterol levels.

Always get a physical check-up from your physician before starting any exercise program.

Additional Exercise Needs for the Stroke Survivor

It stands to reason that someone who has had a stroke needs exercise for the same reasons you do—to reduce tension, fatigue, and depression, to help with weight control, and to lower blood pressure and cholesterol levels.

But in addition, there may be residual effects from the stroke that can be aided by exercise.

Mobility

An early chapter described the passive exercises done by the physical therapist while the stroke survivor is still in the acute care facility. These are done to keep the muscles toned, to prevent joints from freezing or stiffening, and to prevent blood clots.

Even after your family member returns home, exercise is important. If she can walk, encourage her to go with you on what my grandfather used to call a "daily constitutional." It means a regular stroll, through a park, around the block, or even through a shopping center. She may go slowly because of visual problems or difficulties with balance, but you can guide her by gently taking her good arm. Don't rush her.

If the stroke survivor is in a wheelchair, the physical therapist can demonstrate total body exercise techniques adaptable for those in wheelchairs. Don't think that your relative doesn't need exercise because she can't walk. Chances are she needs them even more *because* she is unable to walk.

Expect your relative to have some fatigue when she begins a regular exercise program. As she builds up her tolerance level, the fatigue should become less troublesome. Because most stroke survivors do experience a great deal of fatigue normally, however, you might want to plan a rest period following one of exercise.

Blending Exercise with Other Activities

Ms. Sandy Samberg, a physical therapist at the Howard A. Rusk Institute of Rehabilitation Medicine, NYU Medical Center, suggests other ways in which you can help the stroke survivor to exercise various parts of her body without calling it "exercise," which to many people sounds too much like work. These include:

horticultural therapy

Since 1959 the Howard A. Rusk Institute of Rehabilitation Medicine, NYU Medical Center, has had a garden, a most relaxing spot for patients and their families to stroll through and admire the various plants. New patients are given a plant from this garden for their room upon admission, and many of the plants are sold for profit. But the garden serves an even more important function.

According to Ms. Samberg, stroke patients working in the garden enjoy puttering around in the soil and with the plants. More important, however, their work requires exercising muscles and using small, fine movements—picking up a seedling, placing in into a pot, shoveling soil and moss into the pot, and patting it down. Patients work on balance as well when they grasp large pots or stoop to put them down.

needlecraft and painting

Although many people, including those who are stroke survivors, often consider craftwork nothing but "busy work," it also serves an important exercise purpose. "All creative activities are planned to serve a specific goal, depending upon the needs of the individual patient," said Ms. Samberg. "Painting on an easel may seem like a waste of time at first, until you consider that it offers the patient excellent range-of-motion exercise, especially in moving the shoulder as she paints. It also helps the patient practice balance control as she shifts position to dip her brush into the paint. Even needlecrafts are planned with a specific need in mind. Needlepoint and weaving give hand muscles exercise while at the same time helping eye control. Everything must work together in therapy.''

Activities such as these also offer socializing opportunities, especially if your relative is an outpatient and perhaps misses the company of others who are struggling to overcome effects of a stroke. Many community centers, adult day care centers, church and synagogue groups, and local Y's offer numerous crafts programs for adults. Even if they don't have staff physical therapists, you still may be able to enlist their services in adapting many of their programs for the specific needs of your family member. Chances are there are many other stroke survivors in your community who could benefit from such a program as well.

Follow Doctor's and/or Physical Therapist's Instructions Exactly

It's normal to figure that "if a little is good, more is better." This doesn't hold true, however, when it comes to helping a stroke survivor to exercise. You actually could hurt him by forcing exercises when he is overly fatigued.

Get exercise instructions in writing

Even if you watch the therapist help your family member carry out a particular exercise, it's often difficult to remember exactly what was done when the patient's home and *you're* in charge.

As with other forms of therapy, each part of a stroke survivor's exercise builds toward a specific goal. To be sure you're doing it correctly, ask the doctor or therapist to put the instructions in writing.

Be sure you know not only *what* the exercise is, but also *how many repetitions there are*. If the instructions say the patients should do five leg lifts, rest, and do five more, don't figure ten is better.

Don't "borrow" exercise techniques

Every stroke is different and each person is affected uniquely. The exercises prescribed for your neighbor's mother may be totally wrong for your relative. If in doubt, check with the doctor or physical therapist.

Follow the routine

It's tempting to cut out those parts of an exercise program that are boring, seemingly unimportant, or even painful. But they have been prescribed very carefully for specific reasons.

If you ever saw the movie *The Karate Kid*, you may remember that the youngster was eager to learn karate. Instead his teacher had him first paint a fence, brushing up and down; then he was shown how to wax the car, wiping wax on and then wiping it off, using certain exact hand movements. The boy fumed at this menial labor. Later, however, he discovered that these repetitious movements built up muscles he needed in order to become proficient in karate.

Many of the exercise movements practiced by the stroke survivor have this same purpose—to build up specific muscle groups, to improve range of motion, to help maintain balance for walking, control gripping for self-feeding or grooming. The overall goal of physical therapy is for the patient to regain as much independence as possible. You won't "fool" the therapist by allowing your relative to skip parts of the exercise sequence; you'll be slowing down your loved one's progress.

Continue with the exercise program until the doctor or therapist tells you to stop. Don't let the patient quit because she is bored doing them, hates exercise, or doesn't see any progress or because you think they are a waste of time. They aren't.

Acknowledge Your Feelings

It may come as quite a shock when you suddenly realize that your loved one's stroke has affected you emotionally, stirring up feelings you never knew were there. Part of this flood of emotion comes from shock. One minute your family member was fine, and the next you feared for his life and the quality of that life. Your future, your plans and dreams, may be dramatically altered by your relative's stroke. Daily schedules must be changed, responsibilities shifted, new abilities learned under pressure conditions. If you grew up with illness in your family, those childhood memories and possible fears and resentments may also color your emotions as you now face this present crisis.

Letting Go of Guilt

The burden of guilt is too heavy to carry successfully when you also have to care for a family member who has suffered a stroke. Nothing you did caused your loved one to have a stroke. It's time to let go of the guilt.

Try visualizing guilt as a small bird. If you hold on to it, it will never fly away. Also like a small bird, guilt can dart in and out of your life without your getting a good grip on it.

It's difficult not feeling guilty when someone in your family has had a stroke. You feel guilty about the argument you may have had the day before he had a stroke; you feel guilty that *he* had the stroke, not you; you feel guilty wishing he was like he used to be; you feel guilty wishing someone else could take more of the responsibility for the patient and—dare I mention it?—sometimes you just wish he would die so you could get some rest, and then you feel such over-whelming guilt for thinking such "terrible" thoughts. But they're normal thoughts, all of them.

The road to recovery from a stroke is slow and uncertain. "Patience" is the keyword, for the stroke survivor and family members alike. You should tattoo the word on your forearm, trace it on your bathroom mirror, and write it by the telephone as reminders, because it's so hard to keep remembering. You try to be patient; you encourage, then praise your loved one's successes, no matter how small. Then often, by the next day, the hard-won skill seems lost and must be recaptured. You know the stroke patient is doing his best, but sometimes you feel like screaming. Then you feel guilty. After all, if *you* feel frustrated and defeated, how must he feel?

Caring for someone with a stroke—no matter how much you love them—can be overpowering at times. The pressure and responsibility don't let up. You need to discover ways to relieve some of that pressure, much like a pressure cooker needs its little valve to help blow off some of its steam.

Defusing Anger

If you feel as though you always seem to be mad at someone, you're probably right. Frustration and a sense of helplessness often express themselves as anger. You may feel angry at the hospital or rehabilitation center, at the nurses who didn't come immediately when your relative rang for them, or at the doctor who didn't return your call or answer your questions or who kept you and the stroke patient sitting for two hours in the waiting room. If you catch yourself saying, "I'm so irritated at . . ." or, "I'm just furious about . . .'' ask yourself if your anger is covering up other emotions, such as fear or anxiety.

If the stroke survivor is your parent, you may be angry that you have to parent him now. It's not right. It's not fair. *He's* supposed to comfort and guide *you*. You may be angry when he lashes out at you, saying that you don't help enough or that you're ''no good'' or ''you're just like Uncle Jake'' (who everyone knows was the black sheep of the family).

It hurts. The child in you is being attacked. ''I'm fifty-two,'' a San Francisco architect said, ''and I'm doing my best for my mother. She tells me that I'm an uncaring son, that I haven't done enough, and suddenly I'm ten again and feeling so vulnerable. But I just stand and listen, feeling angry and yet vowing to do better.''

Perhaps you're angry because people—especially your other relatives—aren't behaving as you'd like them to. Have they dumped all the responsibility on you? Not offered to help? Do those who are out of town and therefore not actively involved in the daily care of the stroke patient smother you with ''You should . . .'' and ''Why didn't you . . . ?''

If your anger is stemming from disappointment with the behavior of others, ask yourself some pertinent questions.

Are My Expectations Realistic?

It's easy to want people to behave as *you* think they should behave, not as they do. But most people don't change greatly. Those who always seem to sense what needs to be done usually step right in during a crisis and pick up the slack. Those who have disappointed you in the past probably will do so again. You may be setting yourself up for disappointment and more frustration by expecting people to behave in a way they never have and probably never will.

Am I Willing to Express My Feelings?

If the answer to this question is ''Yes,'' then you need to do it assertively, not aggressively. Tell them how you feel with an ''I'' message, such as ''I feel overloaded with all the responsibility and wish you'd help at least with the medical and therapy appointments.''

Saying, ''You never help me with Dad,'' isn't helpful because it is vague and accusatory. It's more likely to start an argument and create more problems than improve the situation.

Can I Accept That Everyone Handles Stressful Situations Differently?

Your way of handling stress may be to become superefficient and maintain a constant flurry of activity. Your sibling may joke and try to bring humor to the situation. Neither way is right or wrong; each is different. If your sister can't bear to see your father struggle to speak and/or feed himself, let her run errands, pay bills, or interview helpers. We all have strong and weak points. With luck and proper communication, everyone can fill the slot that best suits his or her talents. There's enough work for everyone. Just be sure that you don't always take on the task nobody else wants because ''someone has to do it.'' You'll just end up feeling even angrier. Rather than accepting the martyr's role, see if everyone is willing to draw straws, trade jobs, or otherwise make the work load more equitable.

Does the Stroke Patient Want Only Me to Care for Him?

If so, do I accept feeling trapped because I secretly enjoy the feeling of being needed? Do I refuse help from others because I feel guilty wanting to get away on occasion?

It's important to understand that your actions may make others angry as well. ''My sister resents my leaving for a vacation shortly after she comes from out of town to see Dad,'' a younger brother admits. ''But I do it anyway. It's the only time I can get away and not worry. I've told her that, but she gets upset anyway. I've learned to acknowledge and accept her feelings, and I think she accepts mine, although she doesn't like them.''

A woman caring for three stroke survivors in her home,

her parents and her husband's mother, told of her husband's anger and resentment over her weekly bridge game with her women friends. "I spend one afternoon a week out at one of my friends' houses, playing bridge. Our parents are left with a reliable sitter. They fuss about it, but I know she takes good care of them. I do this for me. If it bothers my husband, it's his problem, not mine. He won't talk about it and won't face that it's unreasonable on his part. I no longer let him make me feel guilty. I look forward to my Wednesdays."

Minimizing Decisions

Anytime a person goes through a traumatic situation, the body's nonessential functions shut down or stage a slow down, protecting the body as a whole. When a loved one suffers a stroke, you also suffer a tremendous blow. As with a death, it takes a while to get over the shock. Your thinking processes and reactions may slow down. You may find it difficult to make decisions or wander from room to room, feeling as though you should be doing something but not being totally aware of what that something is.

Because you're not thinking as clearly as before, you may also become more accident-prone. You may be preoccupied when you drive, taking more risks and driving as though you're on "automatic pilot." Often I found myself at the garage with no memory of having driven there from the hospital.

There's also more potential for home accidents, as I learned firsthand. While still "in a fog," I cleaned out one of my son's closets. (I'm one of those who handles stress best by keeping overly busy.) A can of white enamel spray paint was sitting on a shelf. Almost as a reflex action, I took the can and began spraying the shelves, thinking I'd "freshen them up a bit." In the close quarters, the spray bounced back into my eyes. Although, thankfully, it didn't create permanent damage, I had to be treated for chemical conjunctivitis, adding another series of appointments to my already heavy load of commitments.

Reaching Out for Help

Although there's nothing to be embarrassed about when a family member has a stroke, we sometimes act as though there were. We struggle along, exhausting ourselves and often making ourselves ill as well, rather than admit to others that the load is too heavy to carry alone. It's okay to want help. It's also healthier.

Widen the Family Circle

Although there sometimes are family members who look the other way when you ask for volunteers or a bit of respite, most relatives want to feel needed and are willing to help in some way. Your wanting to "tough it out" may be misunderstood by others.

"I tried to help when Mother had her stroke," a sixty-year-old woman recalled angrily, even ten years after her mother's death. "But my sister insisted on doing it all herself. There were five of us, all willing to pitch in, even my brothers who lived out of state. But Sis wouldn't hear of it. '*I* know what Mother needs,' she said, so eventually we just left her alone. Then she complained that she had all the burden. I think she wanted to be a martyr, so we let her be one."

If you're attempting to do everything yourself, try to understand why. Do you want to "prove" to the stroke patient that you're the most caring? Are you doing it out of some sense of guilt for a long-forgotten (by all but you) mistake? Do you really think you're the only one who can offer gentle and loving care to the stroke survivor? Is it your way of feeling needed? If you really are refusing help from others in your family and don't understand why, consider seeking professional help to find the answers.

Enlist and Enlighten Friends

It is frustrating to want to help a friend in a time of trouble and not know what to do. If your friends ask how they can help, be grateful for their concern and give specific suggestions, such as "Could you stay with Uncle Joe Wednesday morning?" or "Would you come play cards with Dad? It helps him with his numbers and I know he'd enjoy the company."

You'll find that it's easier to coax the stroke patient's reluctant friends to pay a visit if you offer definite suggestions for activities. Some stroke survivors' friends are afraid they won't understand the aphasic or won't know what to say or how to act. Rather than risk feeling awkward or embarrassed, they take the easy way out and don't show up. If you ask them to read a short article or poem aloud, play Scrabble or Chinese checkers, or help with the speech cards, they may feel less anxious and more willing to visit.

If the stroke survivor feels terribly cut off from his former friends and you've had little success getting them to visit, ask them to send him greeting cards, notes, photos, or even cartoons from magazines. Once they've made that effort, it's easier to take the next step, which is a personal visit. You can stay in the room the first time, move away to the porch or kitchen during their second visit, and once they feel comfortable being alone with their friend, you can go for a walk, take a relaxing bath, or otherwise just be "off duty" for a while. It's worth the effort.

Dole Out the Jobs

It may be that you're doing fine with your family member's personal care, practice sessions, and exercises, but you could use help with housework, cooking chores, and errands.

Although there are many services you can hire, volunteer aid is available in most communities to some degree. If you can't afford to hire help, call your local Boy Scouts and Girl Scouts, church or synagogue youth groups, school service clubs, community service clubs, religious service clubs, or your community's social services. See if your community has a Meals on Wheels or other type of home food service program. Sometimes these programs are available only to the elderly, which isn't a great deal of help if the stroke survivor is in his forties or fifties. You also may be able to barter jobs with a neighbor so you cook her dinner or watch *her* patient while she runs your errands.

College students are often willing to do housework for a modest fee to help supplement their spending money. They also might work for room and/or board. As a student I earned extra money reading *The Reader's Digest* a few nights a week to a woman who didn't want to strain her failing vision by reading. Your local college or university or nursing school is also a good source for reliable sitters.

If you're part of the Janus generation—those of us in the middle, parenting our kids in one direction and caring for our parents in the other—you may have just gotten out of the baby-sitter market only to find yourself back in now. It's often far more difficult to find a sitter for a stroke patient than for your child, partly because many people are frightened of the responsibility and more often because, unlike a child who more or less accepts your choice of sitter, the stroke survivor tends to resent his loss of independence and either complains bitterly about your sitter selection or makes life so miserable for the sitter that he or she refuses to return.

Battling Loneliness

It is difficult to maintain your previous life-style, especially if your family member has been seriously affected by his stroke. If you aren't watchful, you can suddenly find your life revolving around the stroke and the destruction it has left behind. Like those whose homes have been destroyed by a hurricane, you can wander around in a daze, wondering, "Why me?" (The answer, of course, is, "Why not?")—or you can take positive steps to having some time to rejoin and enjoy your former companions.

Join or Organize a Stroke Club

Stroke clubs do far more than just offer the stroke survivor socializing opportunities. They also allow the families of stroke patients to meet and mix with others dealing with the same frustrations and guilt. It's not a matter of "misery loves company." You'll find that the mantle of guilt tends to lift a bit when you realize that you're not the only person experiencing a bitter combination of anger, resentment, and resignation when the stroke patient fusses so much when left with a neighbor or paid helper that it's often simpler not to bother trying to go out. It helps to know that others have felt the sense of fatigue so great, that it seems as though you've been doing heavy manual labor. Your life *has* changed, and you'd be suffering from denial if you said otherwise. Meeting with others and seeking solutions is one way to battle the loneliness that comes with stroke.

Retain at Least One Former Activity

Although it's difficult to keep your life as it was before your family member's stroke with all your new responsibilities, hold on to at least one favorite activity with coworkers who knew you before your world caved in and who can talk to you about those interests. It preserves the essence of you, that precious commodity most of us take so for granted. Whether it's some form of exercise, practicing the piano, going to the Elks, or playing mah-jongg, hang on to it. Cherish those moments for you.

Tell Friends What to Expect

Most of us fear the unknown. If you tell friends what your family member *can* do—"He understands everything you say," "He can write simple messages," "He enjoys playing checkers"—you make the terrain more familiar.

Also alert potential visitors to the problem areas—"If too many people talk at once, he gets confused," "He may laugh or cry for no reason, but it passes," "Sit on his right side because he can't see you on the left."

Don't Wait for the Phone to Ring

"Ron's been home for months," a pretty thirty-year-old woman said plaintively. "Friends come to visit, but no one invites us anywhere. I feel as though we're untouchables."

It *would* be nice if friends called to invite you out, either alone, if your relative isn't able to go, or together. But often they won't. People get caught up in their own busy lives. They probably say, "We really should call the Martins and invite them out for dinner." But they don't. Did you, before?

Call your friends to go to a movie. Invite *them* to dinner. Someone's got to break the ice, so it might as well be you.

You'll have to become assertive. If that idea scares you, or you really don't know how, check your local bookstore or library for some of the many books on assertiveness training. One of my favorites is *When I Say No, I Feel Guilty*, by Manuel J. Smith, Ph.D.

Fighting the Sense of Helplessness through Education

Much of the fatigue, anger, and frustration experienced by the families of those who have had strokes comes from a sense of helplessness and fear of the unknown. As important members of your loved one's stroke team, you need to educate yourselves as much as possible in order to understand what has happened to your relative both physically and emotionally, how he reacts, and how the stroke affects you and other family members.

Read everything you can. I've listed a number of books in the "Suggested Reading" section in the back of this book, but there are many more in your library or bookstore. Get a copy of Arthur Kopit's remarkable play *Wings*, which is the tender story of a woman struggling with the aftereffects of a stroke.

Talk to people who have had strokes as well as those who have cared for them. I have tried to include as many anecdotes as possible from people I interviewed, but *everyone* has his or her own story. Not only does stroke affect each person differently, but each of the family members also reacts differently toward the loved one after a stroke. Only by learning from others can we learn about and understand ourselves and our feelings.

Although denial is one way stroke patients and their families handle the overpowering effects of a stroke, eventually we all must accept that, indeed, things *will* be different. Our lives have changed and there's no going back. Knowledge and understanding do help shine some light into what often seems a cavern of blackness. Never accept ignorance; it's a poor companion.

Ask Doctors and Other Professionals Specific Questions

If you ask your relative's doctor, "How soon will he recover?" you're going to feel as though the physician is hedging. And you'll be right. The doctor needs to know your definition of "recover." Is it the ability to function and be somewhat independent? Is it a return to exactly as he was before? Regardless of your definition, however, no doctor can give you an exact timetable. He or she can quote statistics, but that's all they are. Someone is in the 10 percent, while others make up the 90 percent. The best answer you'll get is an educated guess based on many diverse factors.

In the "olden days," the family doctor knew the entire extended family, how they interacted, how members reacted during times of crisis, and who was the "head" of the family. Now you often meet your relative's physician for the first time at the hospital, shortly after your loved one's stroke. The doctor has no idea how supportive your family will be to his patient, how the patient reacts to his family, or how the family will cope with the patient's problems. It puts you both in a "getting to know you" situation.

You can improve communication between yourself and your relative's doctor (as well as the rest of the stroke team) by:

1. learning the terminology and asking specific questions.

"Alan panics so when he chokes on food or saliva," you say to your doctor. "How can we best help him? . . ." or "Mom refuses to do her arm range-of-motion exercises. How much should we push her?" Questions like these permit the caring professional to offer specific and informative replies.

2. making a written list of your questions.

Designate one family member "secretary," to collect the family's questions and present them to the physician, therapist, or social worker. A busy professional wants to answer your questions but may become understandably irritated if each member of a family calls to ask the same question.

3. being pleasant.

Although the professional knows you're under stress, are fatigued, and are frightened, he or she still expects and is entitled to your being civil to the office staff and the professional as well. If your grandmother told you that "you get more flies with honey than vinegar," she was right.

4. reporting symptoms calmly and accurately.

Collect your thoughts before speaking to the doctor. Don't panic or ramble. Get to the point quickly. Don't exaggerate. If Uncle Mark's fever is 100 degrees, don't say it's almost 101.

5. taking notes.

It's hard to remember what the doctor or other professionals tell you when you're under stress. Never apologize for taking notes. Review them often if you're feeling unsure of yourself.

6. admitting when you don't understand.

If you'll speak up when you don't understand an explanation, the doctor or other professional should be able to rephrase it in a different way. It's important that you understand what's going on if you're to help your relative who has suffered a stroke.

Communication is not only vital between you and the professional team, it is also most important among the diverse members of the family. If egos become bruised, try to discuss that issue head-on, so valuable time and energy isn't wasted by a few members of the family engaged in a senseless power tug-of-war.

Develop Communication Lines for Those Out of Town

The out-of-town relatives often feel totally frustrated because they don't know what's going on. "I offer suggestions," said a daughter who lived on the opposite coast from the rest of the family and her mother, who had suffered a stroke, "because no one tells me what's going on. They get angry because I'm also saying, 'Why don't you do this or that?' but if they'd bother to tell me what they are doing, I'd shut up. I just feel so left out of things. It's my mother, too, and I care."

Either form a telephone chain where you call two relatives, who then call two more and so on, or write weekly "progress reports." The time it takes to develop this family line of communication is well worth it. Those other family members care, too, and they may be the very ones who offer to come help so you and the other in-town folks can have some time off. We had one out-of-state relative who was inadvertently left out of the information chain and didn't know my mother had suffered a stroke until many weeks later, when my sister mentioned in a note that "Mother is doing better." Understandably, she was most upset and hurt.

Get Professional Help with Business and Financial Matters

Many people who wouldn't think of treating the stroke survivor without help from a professional medical team think nothing of trying to struggle alone with the business and financial problems that arise, especially when the main wage earner has been taken ill. Someone needs to pay the bills, record and deposit income checks, get bids for household repairs, figure out and fill out confusing insurance forms, and possibly bring in additional income. That someone may be you.

If you have been involved in your own business or have been working a long time, this is just one additional responsibility, but one that can be handled without too much difficulty. If, however, you have never before had charge of the family financial responsibilities, much less even made out a check, this can become a frightening burden. Before you panic, please know that help is easily available.

Many banks have "personal bankers," trained individuals who can sit down with you and explain how a checking account works, how to write checks, and how to balance your monthly statement. They will answer any questions you may have about your checking or savings account and will, of course, treat all information in a confidential and professional manner.

Your credit union also is service-oriented and has a professional staff trained to help you with money-related problems.

For a fee, an accountant or CPA will look over your financial situation and offer suggestions for setting up basic budgets. Many of your community's social service organizations also have specialists who can help you organize what needs to be done. Also check with your area Legal Aid Society. If you qualify for Social Security, contact your local Social Security office. Don't be embarrassed if you don't understand as much as you'd like to about money matters. Most of us don't.

If you're a woman whose husband has suffered the stroke, now is the time to check to see if you have established a credit rating. Many women are shocked to discover that, even after twenty or thirty years of marriage, the credit card they've been using with *their* name on it is, nevertheless, in their husband's name and allows them no credit rating. If their husband should die, they would be unable to use the credit card and might have difficulty getting one in their own right.

Learning What Your Community Has to Offer

The social worker on your relative's stroke team is probably one of your best guides to what your community has to offer stroke survivors and their families. There's no use trying to track these services down by yourself. They can tell you how the U.S. Postal Service "Carrier Alert" program works, where to get emergency calling devices, how to find shared housing, and what respite facilities are available. If they don't know the answer, they usually know where to find them. Save your energy for what you have to do.

If you feel your community lacks a service—such as an adult day care center, Meals on Wheels program, or telephone buddy program (where you arrange for someone to call to check on your relative who is living alone when you are out of town)—then others must feel the need as well. Perhaps your mutual needs can bring together enough people to implement that service for your community. No time? That's how these programs began—by dedicated people who had no time but felt a need, so they made the time.

Developing an Emergency Corps

You'll reduce your anxiety level if you know that you have a second string of helpers lined up, ready to step in if needed. This emergency corps can be a list of names with phone numbers of people willing to sit for a few hours, or drive the stroke survivor to an appointment you can't make, to stay overnight or check on the stroke survivor who lives alone while you are ill or out of town. You are not indispensable; you may even occasionally get sick or want to go away for a weekend. A backup team, trained and standing by, is a necessity, not a luxury.

Also look into nursing homes offering short-term care so your relative can be properly supervised for a week or two while you relax or take a vacation. If you have that information *before* you need it, you'll be more likely to plan a trip and feel less anxious if you become ill.

Your state's Department of Aging can offer a wealth of information. See appendix ''B'' for the address and phone number.

Communicating with Others

It often isn't enough just to acknowledge your feelings; you need to talk about them as well. Friends usually are willing to listen and be supportive, but keep two rules in mind.

Be Honest

Don't play games with your friends. They're not going to hate you if you admit you're tired, angry, frustrated, or resentful. It will do you good to admit those feelings and then go on with life. Denying them just makes them double in size.

Never lie to your psychologist or psychiatrist, either. That may sound obvious, but many people admitted that they didn't tell their therapist how they really felt, because ''it sounded so awful. I didn't want him to think badly of me.''

What a waste of time, money, and effort. Never worry that the therapist will think badly of you. Most likely he or she has heard *much* worse.

Be Brief

When people ask how things are going, they are asking because they either 1) are being polite, or 2) really want to know. If they're just being polite and acknowledging your difficulties, just a ''pretty good'' or ''He's showing some improvement'' will suffice. If it's a friend who you feel really wants to know, you can still be brief. Our troubles are special to us, but even the closest and most special friend doesn't really want to hear a play-by-play from the minute Grandpa got up that morning.

Be honest, say how you feel or how things are, then go

on to other subjects. If things are going well, you'll want to think about other topics, and if they're not going so well, you *should* think about other ones. The old saying, "Smile and the world smiles with you," is, unfortunately, true.

Helping Yourself

Each of us has to do the best we can. No one else can do it for us. Below are a number of ways to help boost your spirits, change negative feelings to more positive ones, and otherwise get more out of life, even though you're dealing with some difficult times.

Exercise

Chapter 11 dealt with the importance of exercise. It is one of the best ways to stay healthy, feel good, and have companionship, if you want it. Even though you may think you feel exhausted, try walking. You'll be surprised how good it makes you feel.

Relaxation Techniques

Just as each of us must find through trial and error the type of exercise we enjoy and can sustain on a regular basis, so must we determine what is relaxing to us. For some people it may be soaring high above the clouds in a glider or soaring through them in a parachute. To me, however, any distance higher than five feet off the ground produces anxiety, not relaxation. I made my husband exchange our college basketball season tickets because we originally were up so high, I couldn't bear to look down to the court.

Music promotes relaxation for many. One of my friends settles onto his lawn chair, shuts his eyes, and lets his entire being become absorbed in the sounds of operatic or symphonic music, courtesy of his extensive compact disc collection. It makes our neighborhood sound very highbrow.

Others relax by painting, soaking in a bubble bath, or practicing one of many different relaxation techniques, such as "progressive relaxation." Although there are many different techniques, progressive relaxation can be achieved, through repetition, by recognizing tension in your body and then relaxing it, either through visualizing a place that seems soothing to you, such as a sunny beach, porch swing, or big feather bed, or by concentrating on a word or phrase. Regular breathing and freeing the mind from everything but the scene or specific word is the key.

"The idea," one expert in relaxation told me, "is not to withdraw from the world, but to be equipped to handle stressful situations by being able to relax and release the tension you feel." Although you first may need to practice relaxation in private, the ideal is to be able to call upon the technique whenever you feel stress, even if it's just while waiting for a traffic light to change.

According to Dr. Thomas D. Borkovec, a psychologist at Pennsylvania State University, daydreams offer another pleasant form of brief relaxation. However, he warns, "Don't replace one habit (such as getting overstressed) with another. Don't get too removed. Daydreaming should never be used as an escape, but rather as a brief release and respite."

Although there are many books on relaxation in the library and your bookstores, the one I prefer is *The Relaxation Response*, by Herbert Benson, M.D. You may find that your stroke patient also benefits from many of these relaxation techniques and that it becomes a special time of sharing for you both.

Massage

Many people, even those who swear they "don't like to be touched," find, to their surprise, that they enjoy having a professional massage. It's been used as far back as the ancient Greeks and Romans for both therapeutic purposes and stress reduction.

There are different styles of massage that vary primarily according to the type and amount of pressure applied. All, however, incorporate some type of stroking and kneading. Sports massage tends to go deep into muscles, while Swedish incorporates quick strokes to the body. It may take some experimenting until you discover which kind you like best. Once you decide, tell your masseur (male) or masseuse (female) so he or she knows what stroke and how much pressure to apply.

You can find a qualified massage therapist through health clubs, by contacting orthopedists or your relative's physical therapist, or through the physical education department of many colleges and universities. If you want someone to come to your home, be sure to get references. Many states require that a massage therapist be licensed before working on clients.

Special Attention to Grooming

It's easy to become so immersed in the stroke patient's routine that you neglect your own personal grooming. You save time and money by not going to the beauty shop, wearing comfortable baggy jeans and a sweatshirt (my favorite work outfit), and not bothering with makeup or, if you're male, with shaving. You wonder why you feel blah. Then you catch a glimpse of yourself in the mirror. You look the way you feel—or is it the other way around?

You'll feel better about yourself and your life in general if you'll spend a little extra time on your personal grooming. Take off that sweatshirt and slip into a brightly colored shirt or sweater; dab on a bit of cologne or after-shave; have your hair done in an easy-to-care-for style; and look in the mirror often. Be proud of your appearance. You'll feel better for it and may find, as an added benefit, that your new look lifts your stroke patient's spirits as well.

Time Off

Most sports offer "time out" periods to give even conditioned athletes a respite. Shouldn't you do the same for yourself? Whether it's time off for exercise, relaxation, reading, or crafts, turning your attention to something other than the sickroom is better for you and for the stroke patient as well. Did you ever think that *he* may need a little time off from you as well?

Maintain Proper Nutrition

With so much else on your mind, eating may lose its priority and become only a necessity. You may grab a candy bar or junk food on the run, letting it suffice for lunch or dinner. After a while, however, your body will start to complain.

Although proper nutrition is always important, it becomes even more so when you are under stress. Stress lowers the body's immune system and makes you more susceptible to illness. Proper eating habits—regular mealtimes, plenty of liquids (preferably water), vegetables and fruits, and complex carbohydrates such as cereals and whole grains can help keep you from becoming overly fatigued and susceptible to infection. Ask your physician if he or she suggests you take additional vitamin supplements while you are under so much stress.

If you aren't certain you're eating properly and want more information about nutritional requirements, contact a registered dietitian or qualified nutritionist. If you can't locate one through your physician or local hospital, write:

> The American Dietetic Association
> 216 W. Jackson Blvd.
> Suite 800
> Chicago, Illinois 60606
> (312) 899-0040

For the names of physicians and clinicians in your area who have received specialized training in the field of nutrition, send a stamped, self-addressed envelope to:

> The American Board of Nutrition
> 9650 Rockville Pike
> Bethesda, Maryland 20814
> (301) 530-7050

Get Adequate Rest

When you first bring your relative home from the hospital, it's usually difficult to sleep well. If she's alone in her own home, you tend to worry. "Is she all right? Could she call me if she had to? What if she's fallen?" Your imagination becomes your worst enemy.

I once called my mother to reassure myself that she was all right. The line was busy. I continued to call at fifteen-minute intervals. It continued to ring busy. Knowing that she had difficulty with her speech and probably would not have been on the phone for over an hour, I called the operator. She confirmed my worst fears. There was no conversation on the line. I tore over to my mother's house, imagining a number of horrible scenes. When I arrived I found her in bed, reading. Her phone had gotten unplugged at the outlet, which, for some reason, made it ring busy. I had trouble sleeping that night.

For those whose family member has moved into their household, there are additional concerns. As with a new baby, half of you tends to stay awake at night, listening for a cry. You sleep, but it often is not a restful sleep. Studies show that "after a year of caregiving, most families reported changes in daily routine and over one-third indicated that their health had suffered."[1]

Fatigue is not always cured by more sleep

Most of the fatigue you'll feel, however, is not cured by more rest. It's a fatigue caused by the weight of responsibility. To some degree it's the exhaustion that comes from hope when progress is made and despair when it is lost or your loved one plateaus. It's the depression that comes from knowing that recovery is slow and, often, imperfect.

Rest your mind as well as your body

Your mind's activity can be every bit as tiring as the extra physical work you are doing—bathing and dressing the stroke

1. M. Adams, M.A. Caston, and B.C. Danis, "A Neglected Dimension in Home Care of Elderly Disabled Persons: Effect on Responsible. Family Members." Paper presented at the meeting of the Gerontological Society, Washington, D.C., 1979.

survivor, running errands, driving to therapy and doctor appointments, and so on. When you aren't actually doing, you may be thinking about what has to be done, mentally making "To Do" lists.

Reread chapter 11 and chapter 12. Make time to get away from everything that is stroke-related, even if it is imaging—going away to a soothing spot in your mind. Exercise your other senses as you imagine the sounds and scents of your mental paradise. Don't feel silly; it works, I promise you.

Some people use pets to help them unwind. Petting your dog or cat or even watching fish swimming lazily around in a fishbowl can be relaxing. The stroke survivor also may benefit from "pet therapy."

Accepting Plateaus

Although there is always hope, at some point you and the rest of the family must accept that there won't be a great deal more improvement, that "what you see is what you get." Having said this—that most significant improvement tends to come within the first six months following a stroke—I must add that many doctors said they saw additional improvement after a year and sometimes even after two or more years.

It's always important to keep encouraging the stroke survivor, but it's unfair to give false hope of returning to "just as you were before." It's important to go on with life, both for the patient and for his family. Accept your loved one as he is each day, for each day is precious and cannot be replaced. If you wait "until Dad walks better" to take him to see the grandchildren, he may never see them. Never postpone life, nor living. Tomorrow is unpredictable.

Even though it's tempting to keep doctor-hopping, hoping that the next one will have some miracle cure, don't waste your time or money. By all means, get a second opinion or even a third, but then allow everyone to get on with this business of living.

Allowing Yourself to Be Happy

In the first chapter I wrote of the power of laughter. It's strong. I believe in it and treasure it as a precious gift from God. It has buoyed me up and carried me along through adversity like current in raging river.

I accept humor, even when I also weep. Recently I visited my father in the nursing home. Although he showed no recognition, he took the banana I offered—one of the few pleasures he still enjoys—and began to peel it. He paused, took a bite, and chewed thoughtfully for at least a minute. Suddenly, as though noticing me for the first time, he said, "Do you want a bite?"

It was a rare moment of lucidity. I wanted to capture it and hold on to it. Tears filled my eyes, "No, thank you," I said politely. "I really don't like bananas."

He nodded and went back to chewing and staring into space. About five minutes passed. Then he shook his head slowly. "No use taking you to the tropics, then," he said.

I burst out laughing. It was a teasing glimpse of the father I remembered. Then I cried.

We, the family of those who have suffered a stroke, have the right to be happy and the need to be happy. Our laughter may also lighten the load for the stroke survivor we love.

"I wait for the other shoe to drop," the daughter of a stroke patient told me grimly. "Mother's blood pressure is still high; her heart's still bad. All the things that triggered the first stroke are still present."

What a waste, I thought. Rather than waiting for the other shoe to drop, go barefoot. Enjoy the warm sand; feel the cool morning dew on the grass; laugh as a kitten licks your feet. Postpone life by waiting? Never.

Find joy in the small victories; take time to cherish the good moments with your loved one; treasure life. Who knows better than we how precious it is and how quickly it may change.

Epilogue

Six months after my mother's stroke and while I was writing this book, my beloved forty-six-year-old brother died suddenly of colon cancer. He left two teenage sons, a wife of not quite two years, and a two-week-old daughter.

My father remains locked in his own world, unaware that his son predeceased him. The shock of my brother's death was, of course, a cruel blow to my mother, who has already had to overcome so much. For a few months, her speech regressed, emotion blocking her laboriously regained ability to form words.

Now, however, she has drawn once again on that mysterious reserve and is able to express her thoughts, haltingly at times, but nevertheless in control.

No, she is not as she was before the stroke. None of us are. But perhaps our priorities are clearer and our love is deeper because we are so keenly aware of how life, as we know it, can be altered in seconds.

There *is* life and love after a stroke. There also is a great deal of learning, as much for the family as for the stroke survivor. We measure days to their fullest now, seeking joy and contentment in our today rather than waiting for any tomorrows. And we keep turning corners to prevent looking back to what was.

Suggested Reading List

After the Stroke by May Sarton (W. W. Norton & Company, New York, 1988).

A Stroke in the Family by Valerie Eaton Griffith (Delacorte Press, New York, 1970).

Can You Hear the Clapping of One Hand? by Ilza Veith (University of California Press, Berkeley, 1988).

Care of the Patient with a Stroke by Genevieve Waples Smith, R.N., M.A. (Springer Publishing Company, New York, 1976).

Episode by Eric Hodgins (Atheneum Publishers, New York, 1967).

Heartmates by Rhoda F. Levin, M.S.W. (Prentice-Hall, Englewood Cliffs, N.J., 1987).

Mainstay by Maggie Strong (Little, Brown and Company, Boston and Toronto, 1988).

Pat and Roald by Barry Farrell (Random House: New York, 1969).

As I Am: An Autobiography by Patricia Neal, with Richard DeNeut (Simon & Schuster, New York, 1988).

Reprieve, by Agnes De Mille (Doubleday & Company, Inc., Garden City, New York, 1981).

Stroke: A Doctor's Personal Story of His Recovery by Charles Clay Dahlberg, M.D., and Joseph Jaffe, M.D. (W. W. Norton & Company, Inc., New York, 1977).

Stroke: The Facts by F. Clifford Rose and Rudy Capildeo (Oxford University Press, New York and Toronto, 1981).

The Road Ahead: A Stroke Recovery Guide, the National Stroke Association, 1420 Ogden Street, Denver, Colorado 80218.

Contacts for Additional Information

American Association of Sex Educators, Counselors and Therapists
435 N. Michigan Avenue, Suite 1717
Chicago, Illinois 60611
(312) 644-0828

The American Board of Nutrition
9650 Rockville Pike
Bethesda, Maryland 20814

The American Dietetic Association
216 W. Jackson Blvd., Suite 800
Chicago, Illinois 60606

American Health Care Association
1201 L. Street, NW
Washington, D.C. 20005-4014

American Heart Association
7320 Greenville Avenue
Dallas, Texas 75231
(214) 373-6300

The American Speech-Language-Hearing Association
10801 Rockville Pike
Rockville, Maryland 20852
1-800-638-8255

Courage Stroke Network
Courage Center
3915 Golden Valley Road
Golden Valley, Minnesota 55422
1-800-553-6321
Membership is $7 and includes subscription to *Stroke Connection*, a newsletter written by and for stroke survivors and their families. This organization also has information on forming stroke clubs and other printed material. Refers callers to their nearest existing stroke club.

National Aphasia Association
Murray Hill Station
P.O. Box 1887
New York, New York 10156-0611

National Easter Seal Society
70 East Lake Street
Chicago, Illinois 60601
(312) 726-6200

National Stroke Association
300 East Hampden Avenue, Suite 240
Englewood, Colorado 80110-2622
(303) 762-9922
They offer a variety of reading material on such subjects as "There Is Sex After Stroke," "The Road Ahead: A Stroke Recovery Guide," and "Therapeutic Recreation."

Newsletter: *A Stroke of Luck*
c/o Helen Wulf
9305 Waterford Road
Dallas, Texas 75218
(214) 321-6804
Newsletter for stroke patients and their families. Small donation is appreciated.

The University of Michigan
Residential Aphasia Program
1111 East Catherine Street
Ann Arbor, Michigan 48109-2054
(313) 764-8440

Visiting Nurse Association of America
3801 E. Florida Ave., Suite 806
Denver, Colorado 80210
1-800-426-2547

══ Appendix A ══

Stroke Rehabilitation Programs

Alabama
Birmingham—University of Alabama Hospitals
Birmingham—Veterans Administration Medical Center
Mobile—Rotary Rehabilitation Hospital

Arizona
Flagstaff—Flagstaff Medical Center
Mesa—Mesa Lutheran Hospital
Phoenix—John C. Lincoln Hospital and Health Center
Phoenix—Maryvale Samaritan Hospital
Phoenix—Phoenix General Hospital
Phoenix—St. Joseph's Hospital and Medical Center
Scottsdale—Scottsdale Memorial Hospital
Sun City—Walter O. Boswell Memorial Hospital
Tucson—Tucson Medical Center

Arkansas
Little Rock—Arkansas Rehabilitation Institute

(Source: American Hospital Association Survey of Medical Rehabilitation Hospitals and Units, 1986. The following information represents a *partial* listing of organized stroke programs offered by rehabilitation hospitals and units responding to survey. Listing does not necessarily imply author's recommendation. Listings in bold print show facilities also accredited in comprehensive inpatient rehabilitation and outpatient medical rehabilitation by the Commission on Accreditation and Rehabilitation Facilities as of May 3, 1989.)

Little Rock—McClellan Memorial Veterans Hospital
Little Rock—St. Vincent Infirmary

California
Arcadia—Methodist Hospital of Southern California
Culver City—Brotman Medical Center
Downey—Downey Community Hospital
Downey—Rancho Los Amigos Medical Center
Fullerton—St. Jude Hospital
Glendale—Glendale Adventist Medical Center
Glendale—Glendale Memorial Hospital and Health Center
Inglewood—Daniel Freeman Memorial Hospital
Kentfield—Kentfield Medical Hospital
La Mesa—Grossmont District Hospital
La Palma—La Palma Intercommunity Hospital
Lancaster—Lac-High Desert Hospital
Loma Linda—Jerry L. Pettis Memorial Veterans Hospital
Long Beach—Memorial Medical Center
Long Beach—Pacific Hospital of Long Beach
Long Beach—St. Mary Medical Center
Los Angeles—Cedars-Sinai Medical Center
Los Angeles—Hospital of the Good Samaritan
Los Angeles—White Memorial Medical Center
Lynwood—St. Francis Medical Center
Marina Del Rey—Daniel Freeman Marina Hospital
Martinez—Merrithew Memorial Hospital
Martinez—Veterans Administration Medical Center
National City—Paradise Valley Hospital
Orange—University of California Irvine Medical Center
Oxnard—St. John's Regional Medical Center
Palo Alto—Veterans Administration Medical Center
Pasadena—Huntington Memorial Hospital
Pomona—Casa Colina Hospital for Rehabilitative Medicine
Red Bluff—St. Elizabeth Community Hospital
Riverside—Riverside Community Hospital
Sacramento—University of California Davis Medical Center
San Bernardino—San Bernardino Community Hospital
San Diego—Sharp Cabrillo Hospital
San Diego—Sharp Memorial Hospital

San Diego—Veterans Administration Medical Center
San Francisco—Laguna Honda Hospital and Rehabilitation Center
San Francisco—Mount Sinai Hospital and Medical Center
San Francisco—R. K. Davies Medical Center
San Francisco—St. Mary's Hospital and Medical Center
San Jose—San Jose Health Center
San Jose—Santa Clara Valley Medical Center
San Leandro—Fairmont Hospital
San Mateo—Mills Memorial Hospital
San Pedro—San Pedro Peninsula Hospital
Santa Barbara—Memorial Hospital of Santa Barbara
Santa Rosa—North Coast Rehabilitation Center
Sepulveda—Veterans Administration Medical Center
Stockton—San Joaquin General Hospital

Colorado
Boulder—Memorial Hospital of Boulder
Canon City—St. Thomas More Hospital
Colorado Springs—Penrose Hospitals
Denver—Mercy Medical Center
Denver—Spalding Rehabilitation Hospital
Denver—Veterans Administration Medical Center
Fort Collins—Poudre Valley Hospital
Pueblo—St. Mary-Corwin Hospital Center
Wheat Ridge—Lutheran Medical Center

Connecticut
Hartford—Hebrew Home and Hospital
Hartford—Saint Francis Hospital and Medical Center
New Britain—New Britain Memorial Hospital
New Haven—Yale-New Haven Hospital
New London—Lawrence and Memorial Hospitals
Wallingford—Gaylord Hospital

Delaware
Wilmington—Medical Center of Delaware

District of Columbia
Washington—George Washington University Hospital
Washington—Greater Southeast Community Hospital

Florida
Bay Pines—Veterans Administration Medical Center
Boynton Beach—Bethesda Memorial Hospital
Fort Lauderdale—Holy Cross Hospital
Fort Lauderdale—Imperial Point Medical Center
Hollywood—Memorial Hospital
Jacksonville—Memorial Regional Rehabilitation Center
Miami—Veterans Administration Medical Center
North Miami—Bon Secours Hospital
North Miami Beach—AMI Parkway Regional Medical Center
Orlando—Florida Hospital Rehabilitation Center
Orlando—Orlando Regional Medical Center
Pensacola—West Florida Regional Medical Center
Punta Gorda—Medical Center Hospital
Tampa—Tampa General Hospital Rehabilitation Center
Titusville—Jess Parrish Memorial Hospital

Georgia
Atlanta—Emory University Hospital
Atlanta—West Paces Ferry Hospital
Augusta—St. Joseph Hospital
Decatur—VA Medical Center Atlanta
Marietta—Kennestone Reg Health Care System
Rome—Floyd Medical Center
Savannah—Candler General Hospital

Hawaii
Honolulu—Queen's Medical Center
Honolulu—Rehabilitation Hospital of the Pacific

Idaho
Pocatello—Pocatello Regional Medical Center

Illinois
Alton—Saint Anthony's Hospital
Belleville—St. Elizabeth's Hospital
Chicago—Grant Hospital of Chicago
Chicago—Holy Cross Hospital
Chicago—Mercy Hospital and Medical Center
Chicago—Ravenswood Hospital Medical Center

Chicago—Resurrection Hospital
Chicago—Rush-Presbyterian-St. Luke's Medical Center
Chicago—Schwab Rehabilitation Center
Chicago—St. Mary of Nazareth Hospital Center
Chicago—VA West Side Medical Center
Downers Grove—Good Samaritan Hospital
Elk Grove Village—Alexian Brothers Medical Center
Galesburg—Galesburg Cottage Hospital
Hinsdale—Hinsdale Hospital
McHenry—Northern Illinois Medical Center
Mount Vernon—Good Samaritan Hospital
North Chicago—Veterans Administration Medical Center
Oak Forest—Oak Forest Hospital of Cook County
Park Ridge—Lutheran General Hospital
Peoria—Methodist Medical Center of Illinois
Peoria—Saint Francis Medical Center
Quincy—Blessing Hospital
Rock Island—Franciscan Medical Center
Rockford—Rockford Memorial Hospital
Urbana—Mercy Hospital
Wheaton—Marianjoy Rehabilitation Center
Wood River—Wood River Township Hospital

Indiana
Columbus—Bartholomew County Hospital
Evansville—Deaconess Hospital
Evansville—Welborn Memorial Baptist Hospital
Fort Wayne—Parkview Memorial Hospital
Indianapolis—Community Hospitals of Indiana
La Porte—La Porte Hospital
Muncie—Ball Memorial Hospital
South Bend—Memorial Hospital
Terre Haute—Union Hospital

Iowa
Ames—Mary Greeley Medical Center
Burlington—Burlington Medical Center
Cedar Rapids—St. Luke's Methodist Hospital
Davenport—Mercy Hospital
Des Moines—Iowa Methodist Medical Center
Dubuque—Mercy Health Center

Knoxville—Veterans Administration Medical Center
Waterloo—Covenant Medical Center-Schoitz

Kansas
Kansas City—University of Kansas Medical Center
Leavenworth—Veterans Administration Medical Center
Topeka—St. Francis Hospital and Medical Center
Wichita—St. Joseph Medical Center
Wichita—Veterans Administration Medical Center
Wichita—Wesley Medical Center

Kentucky
Ashland—King's Daughters' Medical Center
Lexington—Cardinal Hill Hospital
Louisville—Frazier Rehabilitation Center
Louisville—Louisville Baptist Hospitals

Louisiana
Alexandria—Veterans Administration Medical Center
Lafayette—Lafayette General Medical Center
Lafayette—Our Lady of Lourdes Medical Center
Monroe—St. Francis Medical Center
New Orleans—Charity Hospital at New Orleans
New Orleans—Children's Hospital
New Orleans—F. Edward Hebert Hospital
New Orleans—Touro Infirmary
New Orleans—Veterans Administration Medical Center
Shreveport—Willis Knighton Medical Center

Maine
Bangor—Eastern Maine Medical Center
Presque Isle—Aroostook Administration Medical Center
Togus—Veterans Administration Medical Center
Waterville—Mid-Maine Medical Center

Maryland
Baltimore—Church Hospital Corporation
Cumberland—Sacred Heart Hospital
Fort Howard—Veterans Administration Medical Center
Perry Point—Veterans Administration Medical Center

Massachusetts
Beverly—Beverly Hospital
Boston—New England Medical Center
Boston—Spaulding Rehabilitation Hospital
Boston—Veterans Administration Medical Center
Braintree—Braintree Hospital
Concord—Emerson Hospital
Lakeville—Lakeville Hospital
Lynn—Atlanticare Medical Center
Pittsfield—Berkshire Medical Center
Springfield—Mercy Hospital
Woburn—New England Rehabilitation Hospital
Worcester—Worcester Hahnemann Hospital

Michigan
Allen Park—Veterans Administration Medical Center
Ann Arbor—Catherine McAuley Health Center
Ann Arbor—University of Michigan Hospitals
Battle Creek—Southwestern Michigan Rehabilitation Hospital
Chelsea—Chelsea Community Hospital
Detroit—Detroit Macomb Hospital Corporation
Detroit—Rehabilitation Institute
Detroit—Saratoga Community Hospital
Detroit—Sinai Hospital of Detroit
Flint—McLaren General Hospital
Grand Rapids—Mary Free Bed Hospital and Rehabilitation Center
Lansing—Lansing General Hospital
Lincoln Park—Outer Drive Hospital
Marquette—Marquette General Hospital
Midland—Midland Hospital Center
Pontiac—St. Joseph Mercy Hospital
Royal Oak—William Beaumont Hospital
Saginaw—St. Mary's Hospital
Southfield—Providence Hospital
Vicksburg—Bronson Vicksburg Hospital

Minnesota
Madison—Madison Hospital
Minneapolis—Abbott-Northwestern Hospital

Minneapolis—Carondelet Community Hospitals
Minneapolis—Fairview Riverside Hospital
Minneapolis—Health Central Metropolitan Hospitals
Minneapolis—Metropolitan Medical Center
Minneapolis—Veterans Administration Medical Center
Robbinsdale—North Memorial Medical Center
St. Cloud—St. Cloud Hospital
St. Cloud—Veterans Administration Medical Center
St. Paul—United Hospital

Mississippi
Biloxi—Veterans Administration Medical Center

Missouri
Bridgeton—Depaul Health Center
Cape Girardeau—Southeast Missouri Hospital
Cape Girardeau—St. Francis Medical Center
Columbia—Truman Memorial Veterans Hospital
Columbia—University of Missouri Hospital and Clinics
Jefferson City—Charles E. Still Osteo Hospital
Joplin—St. John's Regional Medical Center
Kansas City—Rehabilitation Institute
Kansas City—Research Medical Center
Kansas City—Swope Ridge Rehabilitation Hospital
Kansas City—Veterans Administration Medical Center
Mexico—Audrain Medical Center
Smithville—Spelman Memorial Hospital
Springfield—St. John's Regional Health Center
St. Joseph—Heartland Hospital West
St. Louis—Christian Hospitals NE-NW
St. Louis—Deaconess Hospital
St. Louis—Jewish Hospital of St. Louis
St. Louis—St. John's Mercy Medical Center
St. Louis—Veterans Administration Medical Center

Nebraska
Omaha—Methodist Hospital

Nevada
Las Vegas—University Medical Center Southern Nevada

Reno—St. Mary's Hospital
Reno—Washoe Medical Center

New Jersey
Atlantic City—Children's Seashore House
Camden—Our Lady of Lourdes Medical Center
Chester—Welkind Rehabilitation Hospital
East Orange—Veterans Administration Medical Center
Flemington—Hunterdon Medical Center
Lawrenceville—St. Lawrence Rehabilitation Center
Long Branch—Monmouth Medical Center
Lyons—Veterans Administration Medical Center
Morristown—Morristown Memorial Hospital
Newton—Newton Memorial Hospital
Point Pleasant—Northern Ocean Hospital System
Pomona—Betty Bacharach Rehabilitation Hospital
Red Bank—Riverview Medical Center
Somerville—Somerset Medical Center
Summit—Overlook Hospital
Toms River—Garden State Rehabilitation Hospital
West Orange—Kessler Institute for Rehabilitation

New Mexico
Albuquerque—St. Joseph Health Care Corporation
Albuquerque—Veterans Administration Medical Center
Roswell—New Mexico Rehabilitation Center

New York
Albany—Albany Medical Center Hospital
Albany—St. Peter's Hospital
Albany—Veterans Administration Medical Center
Bronx—Bronx Municipal Hospital Center
Bronx—Montefiore Medical Center
Bronx—North Central Bronx Hospital
Brooklyn—Coney Island Hospital
Brooklyn—Kings County Hospital Center
Brooklyn—Kingsbrook Jewish Medical Center
Brooklyn—Lutheran Medical Center
Brooklyn—Methodist Hospital
Brooklyn—State University Hospital

Brooklyn—Veterans Administration Medical Center
Buffalo—Veterans Administration Medical Center
Castle Point—Veterans Administration Medical Center
Elmira—St. Joseph's Hospital
Flushing—City Hospital Center at Elmhurst
Ithaca—Tomkins Community Hospital
Jamaica—Queens Hospital Center
Johnson City—United Health Services
New Hartford—St. Luke's Memorial Hospital Center
New York—Bellevue Hospital Center
New York—Beth Israel Medical Center
New York—Goldwater Memorial Hospital
New York—New York University Medical Center
New York—Presbyterian Hospital in the City of New York
New York—St. Luke's-Roosevelt Hospital Center
New York—Veterans Administration Medical Center
Northport—Veterans Administration Medical Center
Poughkeepsie—St. Francis Hospital
Rochester—Monroe Community Hospital
Rochester—Strong Memorial Hospital Rochester University
Schenectady—Sunnyview Hospital and Rehabilitation Center
Valhalla—Blythedale Children's Hospital
Valhalla—Westchester County Medical Center
West Haverstraw—Helen Hayes Hospital
White Plains—Burne Rehabilitation Center

North Carolina
Asheville—Thoms Rehabilitation Hospital
Chapel Hill—North Carolina Memorial Hospital
Charlotte—Charlotte Rehabilitation Hospital
Fayetteville—Cape Fear Valley Medical Center
Greensboro—Moses H. Cone Memorial Hospital
Greenville—Pitt County Memorial Hospital
Hickory—Ami Frye Regional Medical Center
Lexington—Lexington Memorial Hospital
Winston-Salem—Forsyth Memorial Hospital

North Dakota
Bismarck—Medcenter One
Fargo—Dakota Hospital

Fargo—St. Luke's Hospitals
Grand Forks—Medical Center Rehabilitation Hospital

Ohio
Akron—Akron City Hospital
Akron—Akron General Medical Center
Akron—Edwin Shaw Hospital
Barberton—Barberton Citizens Hospital
Canton—Timken Mercy Medical Center
Cincinnati—Bethesda Oak Hospital
Cincinnati—Good Samaritan Hospital
Cincinnati—Jewish Hospital of Cincinnati
Cincinnati—Providence Hospital
Cincinnati—Veterans Administration Medical Center
Cleveland—Cuyahoga County Hospitals
Cleveland—Fairview General Hospital
Cleveland—Veterans Administration Medical Center
Columbus—Ohio State University Hospitals
Euclid—Euclid General Hospital
Green Springs—St. Francis Rehabilitation Hospital and Nursing Home
Greenfield—Greenfield Area Medical Center
Lorain—Lorain Community Hospital
Lorain—St. Joseph Hospital
Louisville—Molly Stark Hospital
Middletown—Middletown Regional Hospital
Springfield—Mercy Medical Center
Toledo—Medical College of Ohio Hospital
Troy—Detimer Hospital
Zanesville—Good Samaritan Medical Center

Oklahoma
Oklahoma City—Baptist Medical Center of Oklahoma
Oklahoma City—Oklahoma Teaching Hospitals

Oregon
Eugene—Sacred Heart General Hospital
Medford—Providence Hospital
Portland—Emanuel Hospital
Portland—Good Samaritan Hospital and Medical Center
Portland—Providence Medical Center

Portland—Veterans Administration Medical Center

Pennsylvania
Allentown—Good Shepherd Rehabilitation Hospital
Altoona—Mercy Hospital
Beaver—Medical Center of Beaver City
Butler—Veterans Administration Medical Center
Canonsburg—Canonsburg General Hospital
Danville—Geisinger Medical Center
Darby—Mercy Catholic Medical Center
Doylestown—Doylestown Hospital
Drexel Hill—Delaware County Memorial Hospital
Easton—Easton Hospital
Erie—Saint Vincent Health Center
Harrisburg—Polyclinic Medical Center
Lancaster—Lancaster General Hospital
Langhorne—Saint Mary Hospital
Malvern—Bryn Mawr Rehabilitation Hospital
Mechanicsburg—Rehabilitation Hospital in Mechanics-burg
Philadelphia—Friedman Hospital
Philadelphia—Graduate Hospital
Philadelphia—Hahnemann University Hospital
Philadelphia—Hospital of the University of Pennsylvania
Philadelphia—Magee Rehabilitation Hospital
Philadelphia—Moss Rehabilitation Hospital
Philadelphia—Veterans Administration Medical Center
Pittsburgh—Harmarville Rehabilitation Center
Pittsburgh—Mercy Hospital of Pittsburgh
Pittsburgh—Rehabilitation Institute of Pittsburgh
Pittsburgh—South Hills Health System
Pittsburgh—South Side Hospital of Pittsburgh
Pittsburgh—St. Francis Medical Center
Pittsburgh—Suburban General Hospital
Pittsburgh—Veterans Administration Medical Center
Reading—Reading Rehabilitation Hospital
Ridley Park—Taylor Hospital
Scranton—Allied Service for Handicapped
Sewickley—D. T. Watson Rehabilitation Hospital
Sewickley—Sewickley Valley Hospital
Wilkes-Barre—Geisinger-Wyoming Valley Medical Center

Williamsport—Williamsport Hospital
Wyndmoor—All Saints' Rehabilitation Hospital

Rhode Island
Howard—Center General Hospital
Pawtucket—Memorial Hospital
Providence—Veterans Administration Medical Center

South Carolina
Greenville—Greenville Memorial Hospital

South Dakota
Rapid City—Black Hills Rehabilitation Hospital
Sioux Falls—Johnson Veterans Memorial Hospital
Sioux Falls—McKennan Hospital

Tennessee
Chattanooga—Erlanger Medical Center
Memphis—Baptist Memorial Hospital
Memphis—Methodist Hospital-Central Unit
Memphis—St. Francis Hospital
Memphis—Veterans Administration Medical Center
Nashville—Vanderbilt University Hospital

Texas
Amarillo—High Plains Baptist Hospital
Austin—St. David's Community Hospital
Dallas—Baylor Institute for Rehabilitation
Dallas—Dallas Rehabilitation Institute
Dallas—Presbyterian Hospital
Dallas—Veterans Administration Medical Center
El Paso—Providence Memorial Hospital
Fort Worth—Harris Hospital-Methodist
Fort Worth—Huguley Memorial Hospital
Gonzales—Warm Springs Rehabilitation Hospital
Houston—AMI Twelve Oaks Hospital
Houston—Institute for Rehabilitation and Research
Houston—Memorial Hospital System
Houston—Methodist Hospital
Houston—Rosewood Medical Center
Houston—St. Luke's Episcopal Hospital

Houston—Veterans Administration Medical Center
Irving—Irving Community Hospital
Lubbock—St. Mary of the Plains Hospital
Paris—St. Joseph's Hospital and Health Center
San Antonio—Audie L. Murphy Memorial Hospital
Temple—Olin E. Teague Veterans' Center
Temple—Scott and White Memorial Hospital
Tyler—Medical Center Hospital

Utah
Salt Lake City—Holy Cross Hospital
Salt Lake City—Primary Children's Medical Center
Salt Lake City—Veterans Administration Medical Center

Vermont
Burlington—Medical Center Hospital of Vermont
White River Junction—Veterans Administration Medical Center

Virginia
Alexandria—Alexandria Hospital
Alexandria—Mount Vernon Hospital
Arlington—National Hospital for Orthopaedics
Fisherville—Wilson Rehabilitation Center
Hampton—Hampton General Hospital
Hampton—Veterans Administration Medical Center
Hopewell—John Randolph Hospital
Lynchburg—Virginia Baptist Hospital
Portsmouth—Portsmouth General Hospital
Richmond—Hunter Holmes McGuire VA Center
Richmond—Medical College of Virginia Hospitals
Salem—Lewis-Gale Hospital

Washington
Bellingham—St. Luke's General Hospital
Everett—Providence Hospital
Puyallup—Good Samaritan Community Healthcare
Seattle—Ballard Community Hospital
Seattle—Children's Hospital and Medical Center
Seattle—Harborview Medical Center
Seattle—Veterans Administration Medical Center

Spokane—Deaconess Medical Center
Spokane—Sacred Heart Medical Center
Walla Walla—St. Mary Medical Center
Walla Walla—Veterans Administration Medical Center
Yakima—St. Elizabeth Medical Center

West Virginia
Wheeling—Wheeling Hospital

Wisconsin
Appleton—St. Elizabeth Hospital
Eau Claire—Sacred Heart Hospital
Fond Du Lac—St. Agnes Hospital
La Crosse—La Crosse Lutheran Hospital
La Crosse—St. Francis Medical Center
Madison—Madison General Hospital
Madison—University of Wisconsin Hospital and Clinics
Marshfield—St. Joseph's Hospital
Milwaukee—Sacred Heart Rehabilitation Hospital
Milwaukee—St. Joseph's Hospital
Milwaukee—St. Luke's Hospital
Milwaukee—Veterans Administration Medical Center
Neenah—Theda Clark Regional Medical Center
Oshkosh—Mercy Medical Center
Tomah—Veterans Administration Medical Center
Waukesha—Waukesha Memorial Hospital
Woodruff—Howard Young Medical Center

Wyoming
Thermopolis—Hot Springs County Memorial Hospital

State Agencies on Aging

Alabama Commission on Aging
(205) 261-5743

Older Alaskans Commission
(907) 465-3250

Arizona Office on Aging and Adult Administration
(602) 542-4446

Arkansas Department of Human Services
(501) 371-2441

California Department of Aging
(916) 322-5290

Colorado Aging and Adult Services Division
(303) 866-3851

Connecticut Department on Aging
203) 566-7772

Delaware Division on Aging
(302) 421-6791

District of Columbia Office of Aging
(202) 724-5622

Florida Aging and Adult Services
(904) 488-8922

Georgia Office of Aging
(404) 894-5333

Hawaii Executive Office on Aging
(808) 548-2593

Idaho Office on Aging
(208) 334-3833

Illinois Department on Aging
(800) 252-8966

Indiana Department on Aging and Community Services
(317) 232-7020

Iowa Department of Elder Affairs
(515) 281-5187

Kansas Department on Aging
(913) 296-4986

Kentucky Division for Aging Services
(502) 564-6930

Louisiana Governor's Office of Elderly Affairs
(504) 925-1700

Maine Bureau of Elder and Adult Services
(207) 289-2561

Maryland Office on Aging
(301) 225-1102

Massachusetts Department of Elder Affairs
(617) 727-7751

Michigan Office of Services to the Aging
(517) 373-8230

Minnesota Board on Aging
(612) 296-2770

Mississippi Council on Aging
(601) 949-2070

Missouri Division of Aging
(314) 751-3082

Montana Governor's Office on Aging
(406) 444-3111

Nebraska Department on Aging
(402) 471-2307

Nevada Division for Aging Services
(702) 885-4210

New Hampshire Divison of Elderly and Adult Services
(603) 271-4394

New Jersey Division on Aging
(800) 792-8820 or (609) 292-4833

New Mexico State Agency on Aging
(505) 827-7640

New York State Office for the Aging
(518) 474-4425

North Carolina Division of Aging
(919) 733-3983

North Dakota Aging Services
(701) 224-2577

Ohio Department on Aging
(614) 466-5500

Oklahoma Special Unit on Aging
(405) 521-2281

Oregon Senior Services Division
(503) 378-4728

Pennsylvania Department of Aging
(717) 783-1550

Rhode Island Department of Elderly Affairs
(401) 277-2858

South Carolina Commission on Aging
(803) 735-0210

South Dakota Office of Adult Services and Aging
(605) 773-3656

Tennessee Commission on Aging
(615) 741-2056

Texas Department on Aging
(512) 444-2727

Utah Division of Aging and Adult Services
(801) 538-3910

Vermont Department of Aging and Disabilities
(802) 241-2400

Virginia Department for the Aging
(804) 225-2271

Washington Bureau of Aging and Adult Services
(206) 587-5620

West Virginia Commission on Aging
(304) 348-3317

Wisconsin Bureau on Aging
(608) 266-2536

Wyoming Commission on Aging
(307) 777-6111

Index

Accident proneness, of family members, 185–86
Acute care facility, 52
Age
  as risk factor in stroke, 37
  speech therapy and, 128
Aging, state agencies on, 224–27
Agnosia, manifestations of, 121
American Association of Sex Educators, Counselors, and Therapists, 168
Anatomy of an Illness (Cousins), 19
Anger, 159–61
  brain damage and, 161
  expressing feelings of, 183–84
  of family caregivers, 160, 161, 182–85
  massage and, 160
  of stroke survivor, 159–60
Aphasia
  jargon aphasia, 122
  manifestations of, 34–35, 117–21
  types of, 118–21
Apraxia
  manifestations of, 34, 121–22
  motor apraxia, 122
  verbal apraxia, 121–22
Arteriogram

procedures in, 10
  risks related to, 10
Ataxia, manifestations of, 34

Balance deficit, 141
Bathing difficulty, 151–52
  grab bars, 152
  tubseat, use of, 151–52
Bed sores, 138–39
Birth control, post-stroke, 168–69
Bladder training, 150–51
Blood clots, 139
Blood tests, procedures in, 9
Bowel/bladder difficulties, 149
  bladder training, 150–51
  constipation, 149–50
  preventing accidents, 151
Brain
  and stroke, 25–27, 29–31
  right brain damage, 29–30, 32

Cannon, Walter B., 173
Caregivers
  caregiver application form, 73–74
  checking-up for quality of care, 75–76
  difficulties related to, 66, 74
  evaluating potential helpers, 71–77
  interviewing potential caregivers, 71–72

229

About the Author

Elaine Fantle Shimberg has written books and magazine articles on a variety of medical subjects and is a member of both
the American Medical Writers Association and the American
Society of Journalists and Authors. Her recent book, RELIEF
FROM IBS: IRRITABLE BOWEL SYNDROME was selected
as one of the "Best Lay Medical Books for Public Libraries"
by the *Library Journal*.

Ms. Shimberg resides with her family in Tampa, Florida.

Here's to your Health!!